Protected by Angels

by

DON DICKERMAN

Published by
IMPACT CHRISTIAN BOOKS, INC.
Kirkwood, Missouri

Protected by Angels, by Don Dickerman
ISBN # 0-89228-176-6

Copyright ©, 2004
by Don Dickerman

Published by
Impact Christian Books, Inc.
332 Leffingwell Ave.,
Kirkwood, MO 63122
www.impactchristianbooks.com
314-822-3309

Cover Design: *Ideations*

CONTENTS

PREFACE

If you were attracted to this book by it's title, then you will most likely enjoy reading the book. My motive for writing this book is summed up in the title. My purpose for writing it is to create an awareness of God's presence and His workings in the lives of His children.

All that is written is truth as I know it. There is much exploration of scripture relating to angels. I would like for every believer to be quicker to believe because of this book. I have prayed much before and during it's writing. I will be praying, possibly, as you read, that God's Hand of blessing will touch your heart.

If your child came to you and asked, "Dad, have you ever seen an Angel?" What would your response be? What would it be if he said, "I saw an angel, Dad, ...really!"

This is what this book is all about.

INTRODUCTION

About the time God impressed me to tell of His Holy Angels, many things began to happen in my life. I received news that Billy Graham was writing a book on angels. I was not surprised, and I was convinced He wants the news spread.

I began to notice that many preachers were focusing more on the ministry of angels in their messages. I received a phone call from a lady I had met. A kind elderly lady who later became important in my life. I had talked with her once, and just long enough for us to mention Jesus. Just a few days after my son's sweet experience and my "emersion deeper into His grace," this woman called. She introduced herself, "This is Mrs. Calloway," she said. I remembered her, but was surprised that she remembered me. She said, "If you will come by, I have some books I want to give you." I later found her to be one of God's choice saints, and her life is wrapped up in "giving." What a sweet woman! I went to her home, she gave me a sackful of books and asked me into her kitchen. She offered me a small lunch-coke, cookies, and some fruit. But now God caused a tear of joy to come to my eye, for there on the table was a book entitled, *Angels, Angels, Angels* by Dr. Landrum P. Leavell. This sweet woman gave me the book and rejoiced with me as I shared my reason for being tearfully blessed. Isn't God good!

I didn't need much more incentive to write the book. But it seemed confirmations were all about me.

FOREWORD

I have just completed a wonderful journey while reading through Brother Don's manuscript about "Angels." My wife and I work among the Muslim's on the red clay plains of Uganda, East Africa. In 2001, I was at a missionary fellowship in Jinja, Uganda. We were enthralled for several hours to hear missionary testimonies about great angelic deliverances. Stories of protection from dictators, soldiers, angry mobs, and wild animals declared the love of God for his kids. Divine Interventions which are still happening today! This book is an intervention testimony about the ministry of angels. It could rightly be called "The Current Chronicles of the Glory of God."

Years ago, Brother Manley Beasley was at death's door. During that difficult hospital stay the Lord encouraged Manley with a vision of heaven and the ministry of angelic messengers. A year later, and just a few days before his death, I flew with him and his wonderful wife Marthe from Lubbock to Dallas. Manley had several bandages over amputation wounds that once had been fingers. Lesions in his throat made it impossible to drink water. All he could do was suck on a few ice chips. He was in real pain, yet he seemed to be in real peace! "Brother Manley? You told us to "Count it all joy" when we suffered. You said that the Lord would meet us at the point of our need with his peace. Have you found that to be true? Have you gotten to that "Count it all joy" place yet, through all of the pain you have endured this year? He smiled and said, "Son, I'm not there yet, but I'm getting close." His answer blessed me so much that it gave me the courage to ask him about the vision of angels and heaven. I said, "Please encourage me again! I heard about a heavenly glimpse of glory the Father gave you last year." "Brother Manley, please tell me what you saw!" I held my breath waiting for his story. "NO", he said abruptly! "I can't tell you what I saw!" Instantly despair filled my soul. "Why not," I cried? He paused for a moment and then said gently, "Son, if I tell you what I saw, you will start living by my word instead of His. Your heavenly Father wants you to live according to His word, not mine!"

He was exactly right. That is why I willingly endorse this book. It belongs in your hand because it declares God's word concerning the current ministry of angels. It is a "glory shout," a Holy declaration that God loves us and is still intimately involved in every detail of our lives. Every page is a confirmation of Jesus words in Hebrews 13. Do you remember them? Heb. 13:5-8 ... *for he hath said, I will never leave thee, nor forsake thee. So that we may boldly say, The Lord is my helper, and I will not fear what man shall do unto me.*

This book is for those that have lost their heart or misplaced their faith, or feel they've been left alone. Just before John Baptist lost his head in Herod's court, the greatest man born of woman (according to Jesus), needed a confirming word that Jesus was really the Messiah. Matt 11:2 tells us that Jesus sent word and said, "Tell John that the blind see, and the lame walk." This is a word that Angels still fly! This is a word that the ministry of angels is not over. Father God speaks encouragement through these pages to all that have grown faint of heart. He that has begun a good work in you will complete it, even unto the day of the Lord.

Look up dear heart, your redemption draweth nigh. He is coming on a white horse surrounded with His **Holy Angels.** I believe if you will look closely, you will see they are already here, and Jesus is standing at the door!

Missionary/Evangelist John Karl Davis

Chapter 1

MEMORIES OF MINE

Luke 1:11 *And there appeared unto him an angel of the Lord standing on the right side of the altar of incense.*

I approached my fellow office workers one morning with my usual greeting of "Morning, men" but in the back of my mind, I had something about to burst forth which I had to share. I took my seat at my desk and was caught up in the small talk with friends prior to the 8:00 a.m. hour. My heart wanted to tell of an experience with angels, God's Heavenly messengers, but I felt they would not believe me. I thought I would be ridiculed and laughed at, like those who see "spaceships."

Still, some of these men were Christians; they read and believe God's Word. They trusted Jesus for salvation, had a prayer life; why not share this most unusual experience with them? Perhaps they would be blessed. I was convinced that I must share what God had done in my life the night before.

So, I began to tell of an "angelic experience" which I will relate later. They listened. Soon they began to look at each other with a look that betrayed their false interest. I could detect that they did not believe it, and were skeptical about

1

God's Holy Angels still ministering today. I did not want to share any more. The experience was too sacred to share in the midst of the obvious unbelief and doubt. It was like casting pearls before swine. They were not able to appreciate the value of what I had to share. I can understand their reaction as just a few days before I might have reacted similarly. As I address my readers, let me first address the skeptics.

I guess there are two kinds of people, those who divide people into two categories and those who don't. I fall in the former. I believe Jesus separated men at Calvary into two groups, believers and unbelievers. In the category of believers there are those who are negative and skeptical about anything "they" themselves have not experienced. And there are those who are ready to believe God. Those whom, by faith in His Word, are willing to accept the outpouring of His grace and love.

Skeptics sent Jesus to the cross, though He voluntarily "laid down His life" for man's redemption. Let me distinguish between cautious, careful discerning of the spirit, and skepticism. Skepticism, I believe, is seldom based on scriptural knowledge. Instead, it is the product of scriptural ignorance. Skepticism says, "show me" a sign. Jesus assured the Jews that there would be no sign given other than an empty tomb. "As Jonah was three days and three nights in the whale's belly . . . (Matt. 12:40)." Thomas demanded to see and touch Jesus before he would believe. Jesus said, "Blessed are they who believe and have not seen." (Paraphrased). Ordination by man is only meaningful if it is backed up by God's ordination. I suppose there are many who have been ordained by man that are not recognized by the Lord Jesus. Many have book knowledge and yet are still spiritually ignorant of the workings of the Holy Spirit. Many have limited the working of God in their life because of "skepticism." Most skeptics are quick to let you know they are not skeptics. Those who do not believe in the "supernatural" will find little benefit from reading this material. God is pleased by FAITH.

To enter God's kingdom, faith is a requirement (Eph. 2:8-9). To be let down deep into God's storehouse of blessing, faith is a requirement. "Without faith it is impossible to please him . . . " (Heb. 11:6). The birth of Jesus was supernatural and God's *marvelous messengers were* put into action by their Creator, becoming an important instrument in the Manger Mission. The increase in angelic activity around the birth of Christ is similar to what we may well experience at His Coming. Doubtless, there is an increase in angelic activity and manifestation.

The word angel means, "Messenger." They might be correctly referred to as "God's Holy News bearers."

Somewhere back in God's history, nothing existed but the Holy Trinity. I cannot give you the sequence in which the "things" of God's universe were created. However, by believing God's Word, I do know that all things were created by and for Jesus (Col. 1:26-28). The angels existed before man and they witnessed man's creation. They were created as super-intelligent beings and much of God's will was revealed to them. The entire book of Revelation attests to this. I knew very little about the Holy angels of God prior to the experience I am about to share.

3

My oldest son Donnie came to know Jesus when he was 8 years old. He was exposed to the Gospel more than the average 8-year-old, but he trusted Jesus because he realized he was a sinner and Jesus is the Savior. He came to Christ just as everyone else who is born-again. Everyone that is saved today is saved the same way. I am proud of my son, Donnie. He learned to love Jesus at an early age and he brought several of his friends and, ultimately, their families to know Jesus as a third grader. I am happy that he grew up loving Jesus and sharing Him with others. Both of my sons were typical boys 3-years apart. They played football, baseball, basketball, and even fought with each other occasionally. What I want you to understand is that what I am about to relate to you happened to a perfectly typical 7-year-old boy, my youngest son, Robby. Robby is now a neurosurgeon but when this experience took place he was in the second grade.

"I saw an angel Dad really!" Robby, our youngest son, had been saved about a year when this happened. He, like his older brother, trusted Jesus at an early age. They were not prompted. They came to Jesus, convicted by the Holy Spirit. From the time Robby was very young he had difficulties with allergies. He was often sick because of his condition and it had become apparent to me a few months prior to this experience that it was allergies that troubled him. Now, I identified with this because I also had allergy problems. I empathized with him; I prayed for the Lord to heal him, prayed for him as I had for no one else.

As I met Christians throughout my daily walk I would ask them to pray for my son. I had met some real "giants" for the Lord and many, many prayer warriors were lifting up his name to God's Throne. I had an appointment to see an ear, nose and throat doctor on October the 7th to see if a cyst he had located in my sinus cavities needed to be removed. This was in February; my appointment was made eight months in advance. In the meantime, my wife and I had decided to have Robby examined by an allergist. Now, you may wonder why I mention this, but I think you will value the result. The doctor Robby was to see was located in the same building as my doctor and our appointments were for the same date, 15 minutes apart.

This was pure coincidence, or you may prefer to believe God had something to do with it. Personally, I do. I had prayed so much for my son that I was confident he would be healed. That day, before I left for the doctor's office, I went by to see Francine Morrison, a great gospel singer and a spirit-filled believer. She loved to pray for folks. I told her about Robby and we had prayer together. She prayed for me to be healed also and gave me her latest recording called, "Rise and Be Healed." That day I pushed aside all traditional training and, as best as I knew how, I released my faith to God!

After the doctor examined me, he inquired, "What kinds of medicine have you been taking?"

"Just the antihistamines that you prescribed," I said.

He shook his head and said, "They don't remove cysts. However, I cannot find the one you had earlier. It is not there. I see no need for me to treat you further!" He looked at me and said, "I'm sorry, I must have probed a little hard (tears were in my eyes)."

"No," I said, "God is just so good, I can't hold them back."

"I am not surprised," he said, "I would hate to think I was treating patients alone." He acknowledged God's power. I almost ran to the office where my son was being examined. I knew he was going to be healed. I arrived, as the skin tests were being completed and learned that he was very allergic. As the doctor talked, my heart dropped. He told me of special equipment Robby would need which would cost $2,500. I walked from the office "doubting," but only for a fleeting moment!

God had healed me and I doubted His provision for Robby. My prayer for Robby was not answered the way "I" wanted it answered, but God had heard my cry, just as he had Daniel's in Daniel, chapter 10. The answer was on the way!

The very next evening when I arrived home from work, men were there to make bids on installing the equipment. However, it was Wednesday and I needed to go to church. I excused myself, but before I left Robby came to me and said, "Dad, can I go with you?" He had not had supper and because of the circumstances, I told him to stay home with Mom and Donnie. He said, "Wait, Dad, I'm going out in the backyard under that tree and read my Bible, where does it talk about my angels?"

I thought a moment and told him to read Matthew, chapter 18. He was only seven and could barely read, but he went out with his Bible as I left. After church, several people wanted to talk, some had problems, and others had

6

just wanted to talk. It was past Robby's bedtime when I finally got home, but he was up and waiting. He had made arrangements with his mother to sleep with me because "he just wanted to talk."

God's spirit still was very heavy upon me after the experience the day before. His presence was very real. Robby and I went to bed. The lights were out and my wife and other son were asleep in another room. I asked Robby what he wanted to talk about. He said, "Dad, have you ever seen an angel?" I told him no, that I never had. He said, "I saw an angel, Dad-really! I saw two of them. While I was reading my Bible under the tree, I asked God if He would let me see 'my angels' and He did!" This caught me by surprise and I began to cautiously question him. He sensed the doubt in my questions and he began to cry. Through his tears he said, "I knew nobody else in the whole world would believe me, but I thought you would." Then he said, "Dad, they are here, they are in the room right now and they look sad."

I saw nothing even though there was enough light to see the doors and windows. However, I did sense an awesome presence of God! I explained to Robby that I could not see them, but assured him that I believed he did. I asked where they were and he said that one was standing at the door and the other one right beside him. I was careful not to put words into his mouth but asked if they were small like little statues that he may have seen. "Oh, no, Dad. They are bigger than you, they're bigger than the door." I asked if they had long blonde hair and looked like women, because I thought maybe he had seen paintings like this. "No, sir, one of them has dark hair and one has blonde hair, but it is short and

7

they're not girls, they're men."

I became increasingly more aware that God was letting him see what millions of Christians never get to see. Robby was not afraid, nor surprised. He told me, "I just knew God would let me see them 'cause he knows how much I love Him and how much I wanted to see "my angels." I asked him if he could describe them to me, and without hesitation or forethought, he said, "The one at the door is big and has short blonde hair and looks kinda like Uncle Dick in Georgia. He has either two big wings or six little ones. I can't tell for sure, it's sort of foggy but I believe he has three wings on each side, they sort of cover up his arms and he has a black book in his right hand, nothing in his left hand." I asked if he had on a gown and, Robby said, "No, he has on really shiny white clothes, kinda like those soldiers wear in pictures. His belt is shiny white." I asked if he could see the angel's feet. He rose up in bed and said, "Yes, sir, he has on sandals laced up around his legs."

I asked about the angel standing at his side and he giggled a little in excitement. "He looks kinda like me Daddy, 'cept his hair is dark and he is a man." He asked me if they would play with him and I told him no, they were sent from God to watch over and protect him. I told him they only wanted him to worship God.

"Every time you say Jesus or God, they look at you and smile," said Robby. I asked if he would describe them further. "Yes, he has either two big wings, or four little ones." He just couldn't be sure. He said it looked like little lines on their wings, but it wasn't really clear. "He has a sword in his right hand and a little red Bible or book in his

8

left hand. His clothes are the same. They are really shiny white, Dad, really white."

He asked me if he could go with them. "Go with them?" I could barely hold back my tears; had God sent His angels for my son? I asked him why he wanted to go with them. He said, " 'Cause they're so pretty and I want to watch over you and Mom and Donnie, so no one will ever hurt you." I explained to him that he could not be an angel because God has something better prepared for His children. He said, "They're smiling again, Dad." Then he asked if he could talk to them. I really didn't know what to say because I had never seen an angel before, but I told him he could try. He turned to the one by his bedside and asked, so sweetly, "What's your name?" He said the angel replied either Judas or Jude. Robby seemed alarmed and asked if Judas wasn't a bad man. I explained to him that many other people were, named Judas, or Jude, beside the one who betrayed Jesus. I knew my son would have never made up that name. This was very real.

He then asked the one at the door for his name and told me, even though he could barely hear, he was sure it was Daniel. This experience lasted for about three hours. He asked me if he could touch them, again I said, "Rob, I just don't know. If you want to try, I will go with you." He said, "I think they will come to me if I ask." He asked in 7-year-old faith, "Daniel will you come to my bed so I can touch you?" He was elated, immediately he said, "Dad, feel how soft their wings are." He took my hand and directed it, but I felt nothing–nothing but God's presence in a way I had never known before.

Soon he said, "I don't need to see you anymore tonight, but please stay and let me see you when I wake up." In a few minutes he was asleep, but not me. I could not sleep. I had been bathed in God's love and grace. I had experienced something that made me aware of God's presence as never before. I listened for God to speak to my heart. It was as though He was saying, "Go and tell the world about my Holy Angels." I could not recollect hearing a message or preaching a message on God's supernatural beings. I was sure if I had seen angels, I could not speak or write of them. It was not necessary to my faith to see them, but how it increased as I witnessed them working in my son's life. I could tell of their activity and ministry today with great assurance even though I never have seen an angel.

The next morning, as I arose to leave for work, I went to the bedside to kiss my sleeping son. I realized I was standing where one of "his angels" stood, or was standing. He opened his eyes, and said, "I love you, Dad." He looked around the room and said, "Dad, they're still here." He smiled and closed his eyes in the sweetest experience I have ever known since my walk with Jesus began.

In the following weeks and months I had read more about angels than ever before. I had interviewed numerous people and had checked every detail my son related with God's Word. There was no conflict, but rather abounding evidence. He has told me, and only me, (he would not talk about the angels to anyone else), of a few occasions where they have appeared to him since that night. Once as he was taking a test at school, he said he was getting confused and was about to cry. He said, "I knew the answer, but my mind wouldn't think." Just before tears came, his angel Daniel appeared and said simply, "Now think, Robby," then the angel disappeared. "Dad, he didn't tell me any answers, but my mind got smart again." He told me that once, as he ran outside to recess, there were two groups of kids playing. As he started toward one, Daniel appeared in front of him and said, "Don't go over there, Robby. You will get hurt." He said he has seen them a few times when his mother drove him home from school.

"Daniel always stands outside of mom's (car) door and Judas by mine. They don't fly, they just go beside the car." On another occasion, he told me of being in our backyard playing. "Mom called me once to come in, but I didn't go," he said. "Daniel came and stood in front of me and said, 'Go on in now, Robby.'" He often sees them on the school playground, standing beside a tree watching him. Now, I know there will be some who read this who will not believe it. My purpose for sharing this is not for you to believe it, but to believe God! Believe Him, believe His Word, believe that His "angels are ministering spirits sent forth to minister for them who are heirs of salvation." I will give you scriptural reasons why I believe this and give some accounts of how God opened my eyes of faith.

The Scripture says in Matthew 18:10 "Take heed that ye despise not one of these little ones; for I say unto you, That in heaven their Angels do always behold the face of my Father which is in Heaven." The reason I wrote this is all contained in this one chapter. I have been a Christian for many years and I have had some wonderful experiences with My Lord and Savior. However, I have never seen an angel. I have heard "faint sounds," as though God opened Heaven's doors and let me listen in, but I havenot seen an

11

angel.

When I was 19 years old, I felt God's hand upon my life. I vividly recall walking the aisle of the Victory Baptist Church in Fort Worth, Texas. God's touch and call on my life are still very alive! I gave all of myself that I knew how, to all of God that I understood that night. I told God through tears that came from deep in my heart that I would do anything He wanted me to do. That impression has not dimmed. The visiting preacher that evening spoke on Baalam; he mentioned the angel that appeared and the donkey (Numbers 22). He said, "Even a dumb animal can recognize his own master." I then realized that I needed to allow Jesus to be Master of my life. That night I did!

After that night I began to feel that God wanted me to preach, but I could name many reasons why that could not be. I was bashful, sort of some typical Moses type reasoning. I could not even give a book report in school. Also, athletics had been my life, and now I was a college freshman anxious to play college basketball. Each night, as I prayed and told Jesus that I loved Him, my heart felt a tug to turn loose of my life and let Him have it completely. I read my Bible late each night, and would look out my window unto the Heavens and ask God for a sign. A falling star, an odd-shaped cloud, just something from Heaven, to let me know He wanted me to preach. Basketball practice had started at college. I was even more confident in my ability after looking at the competition. I thought I was the best guard on the squad (I am not boasting, but leading to a point). The coach was away the first few weeks of practice and only the trainer and team captain were there to see me practice.

A few days before our first game the coach returned and explained that, since he had not been there, he was only going to use the players from last year's squad. He told me and another freshman that he would like to "red-shirt" us for a year, meaning we would work out with his squad but, but if we played in any games, we would lose a full year of eligibility.

I understood, I guess, because God was still dealing with my heart to preach. Inwardly I had said, "When I finish basketball, I will preach." It was increasingly more difficult for me to swallow being "red-shirted." I worked out with the team and beat the best guards on the team. About mid-season the coach asked me to join the squad as starting guard, meaning I would play 8-10 games and lose the full year of eligibility. I sought the Lord for guidance and it seemed difficult for me to pray about basketball. I suppose I was getting my priorities somewhat in order.

God gently reminded me that I had given my life to Him and I was able to see that basketball was not that important. I had no problem deciding what to do. That night I gave the thing I lived and worked for to Jesus. I gave Him my life, and told the coach that I no longer had a desire for basketball. God removed the desire to play and put something better in my heart, a desire to live just for Him! As I prayed and praised the Lord, for hours it seemed, I heard "something" which I will call heaven's approval, for lack of a better description. What I heard is totally indescribable and I couldn't talk about it even if I felt impressed of God to do so.

God is so good.

14

Chapter 2

MISTAKEN MYTHS

I Corinthians. 6:3 *Know ye not that we shall judge angels? How much more the things that pertain to this life?*

Angels have been in existence since before the creation of man. How long before man's creation, no one really knows. Angels exist in the minds of unbelievers and even apart from Scripture or known revelation from God, angels have been a part of man's thinking. Perhaps the most difficult thing in understanding God's Holy Beings is putting aside all of the non-scriptural accounts of angels. I will reiterate here that my reason for believing in angels is not, having seen them, nor hearing them, or having been touched by one. I believe in them because God's Word teaches their existence very clearly.

I grew up thinking of angels mostly at Christmas time. I can recall numerous instances as a child singing "Hark, the Herald Angels Sing." I pictured in my mind feminine looking, white robed, blonde-haired creatures with bird-like wings and funny looking trumpets, singing all around Bethlehem. I could envision their shining halos while they sat on clouds, singing to all Israel about the newborn Jesus.

Bible study caused me to push almost all of these ideas aside. Perhaps the angels did sing, but the Scripture does not say so. The so-called "angelic choir" is not found in God's Word. I personally believe the angels do sing. If they did sing on that night, it was not to all Israel or even all Bethlehem, but rather to the shepherds. What they did do was to announce His coming while praising God. I do not believe we err seriously to say that the angels sing. Certainly no more melodic words have ever fallen upon the ears of man. My point here is that tradition is often not in total agreement with Scripture.

Admittedly, there is little taught about these Holy creatures. Sunday school teachers have been remarkably quiet; the pulpits have been silent! Two preachers felt led to write books on angels: Dr. Landrum P. Leavell and Billy Graham. Both men made this statement in their books, "I do not ever recall hearing a sermon on angels." As I read that statement, I looked back over my Christian life and realized that I, too, had never heard a sermon on angels. I was immediately impressed of God to find out why. I began to study, and I believe at this point it is necessary to determine:

What angels are not! First, they are not some kind of *"feminine creature "* with bowed heads and strange looks upon their faces. The Bible gives no indication of angels being feminine, but rather implies they are masculine, as we understand masculinities. They are powerful. They appear throughout the Scripture in the form of men. They bear names of men, Michael, Gabriel. Without being repetitious, let it suffice at this point to say that angels are not feminine in character. A later chapter will deal with this.

The angels are not *saints who have died!* Somewhere in man's thinking this seemed to be an appealing thought, but again, it is contrary to Scripture. Christians do not become angels. They receive a glorified body and will ever serve the Lord as His redeemed, blood-bought creation. 1 John 3:2 " . . . we shall be like him . . ."

Angels are *not all good.* In man's conversation, almost every reference to an angel is good. Again, the Scripture is clear on the subject, depicting fallen angels, demons who are part of Satan's host of powers and principalities. Husbands who refer to their wives as angels do so as a compliment and term of endearment. No man with an understanding of Scripture wants an angel for a wife. They are non-feminine, powerful, non-reproductive, and not necessarily good. Not all angels are Holy angels.

I have yet to find Scripture that describes the "halo" all angels traditionally have. Whether or not they have halos is not really important. It is important that we put aside all that is not in God's Word. His Word will be true to us. His Spirit will give us understanding as we seek to know more about His Holy creatures. Make sure the Holy Word of God justifies the faith that you have placed in religious tradition.

Angels are *not all alike.* Their descriptions throughout God's 66 books are many and varied. They do *not all have the same power.* Angels are *not funny-looking, little chubby, red-faced babies with wings.* Man has somehow chosen to picture this silly-looking little creature as the

17

Biblical cherub. No!

The cherubim (plural) were placed as guards at the Garden of Eden with flaming swords (discussed in a later chapter). The Bible gives no account of fat little baby angels.

The angels are immortal, in other words, they will live forever. Therefore, they are not aged. They do not desire man's worship. They are *not emotionless robots.* Some willingly rebelled against God. They are *not without freedom of choice.* This is evident just in the fact of "fallen angels." Any believer with an inkling of Bible knowledge knows that God did not create anything bad. At one time there were only Holy angels. For some reason, a host of angels rebelled against God.

Some angels have fallen as many say. But I believe fallen is a weak word to describe what happened. They didn't fall out of heaven. They were kicked out, cast down to the earth. Lucifer was the leader of these rebels. God created them with choice, and our only reason for discussing this now is to understand that angels are not "puppets" of God. They are not machine-like creatures, but they do move at His direction.

Angels are not omniscient and do not have full knowledge of God's plan and program. They are intelligent beings, but they are finite. That attribute belongs only to God. God apparently created them to share in His Counsel and Wisdom, for they help carry out the plan and will of God. Still, it is important to remember that their intelligence, though greater than man's, is limited.

The angels are not able to act without God's direction. This is an assumption well supported by Scripture. They move as His messengers, His holy deputies, at His command. The angels sent to destroy Sodom and Gomorrah could not act until Lot and his family left the city. This is a beautiful picture of the rapture of the church. Angels cannot "fall" again; it seems there is a parallel to the Christian life here. The angels made a choice before man's creation and it appears that the choice is locked-in for eternity.

Of this, we can be sure; the fallen angels can never be Holy angels, just as the rich man could not return from Hell. The fallen angels are in " . . . chains of darkness, to be reserved unto judgement" (2 Pet. 2:4). This Scripture seems to indicate that it is "as good as done," because certainly the fallen angels (demons) are active in the world today.

As a matter of Scriptural fact, 1 Corinthians 6:3 indicates that Christians will judge angels, certainly not the Holy angels but the fallen angels, that "sinned" against God.

The angels are not our servants, they are God's! They are ". . . ministering spirits, sent forth to minister for them that shall be heirs of salvation" (Heb. 1:14). Yes, angels minister "for believers," not "to" them, but only as they are *"sent forth "* from God. (The angels are not bodily in form, though they may take on such form.) They are spirits and fit in the realm of the invisible principalities and powers. Jesus clearly gave us authority in "loosing and binding" spirits. I believe that not only includes authority, in the Name of Jesus Christ, to bind evil spirits, but to also release Holy Angels to minister for us.

19

Angels do not obey man; and they cannot intercede in prayer. Jesus is our Intercessor! Angels may come to answer the prayers of believers, but only as directed by God. They do not desire any of the glory that belongs to God.

Perhaps you expect to read somewhere in here that angels are not active today, that their earthly ministry ended somewhere in times past. I will speculate as to why I believe man knows little about the ministry of angels.

When the fires of persecution and martyrdom flamed around God's children, believers related stories of angels intervening. However, in today's age of plenty we have become *less* dependent upon God. We have become educated enough to rationalize the super-natural, and to some degree, pride ourselves on being self-sufficient. We do not look for, nor expect, the ministry of angels. Faith has dwindled as man's knowledge has increased; as luxury came, so did independence from God. God has not changed! Nor will He! The angels have not changed! Their creation purpose is the same. The assignments given them by Jehovah God have not changed. We have!

The angels are not gone! They stand ready to minister. Of all the things they are *not, they* are not gone!

Satan has made an attack upon every Biblical doctrine, his purpose being to deceive or confuse believers or potential believers. Giving credit where credit is due, Satan has done a good job of confusing man concerning God's supernatural creation. As he has done with salvation, he has split believers into groups called denominations–many denominations, which take the same Bible, and teach as truth, doctrines of error. Satan can transform himself as an Angel of Light; and he has his "own" messengers in the pulpits II Corinthians 11:13-14). So it is not surprising that beliefs about angels are as wide and as varied as denominationalism itself.

If Satan could deceive the "elect of God" he would have you disregard "his" fallen angels and God's Holy Angels. He would have you "explain away" the supernatural. In our brilliance we can also be astoundingly stupid. Why are we more ready to doubt than to believe? Why do we keep our emotions within when worshiping? If God rings joy bells in your heart, should He not be praised? I recently spoke at length with a hospital chaplain. I questioned him concerning angels in his ministry. He told me of a man who was "clinically dead" because of a cardiac arrest. The blood was not moving through the man's body, and his heart was not working. After about three minutes, the chaplain explained, the doctors succeeded in reviving the man.

The chaplain told me that the man, though his mind and body were clinically dead, had heard every word spoken by the doctors and attendants while they frantically worked to bring life back to his body. He also said he saw his mother and father (long before deceased), standing at the foot of his bed. He further stated that he did not want to "come back." He had seen something so beautiful and peaceful that he wanted to "go on in."

"The mother and father at the foot of his bed," I said, "how do you explain that? Were they really angels in the form of his mother and father?"

The chaplain responded by saying, "I really don't know how to explain it. It may have been his deceased parents coming to escort him into heaven, and it may have been angels." However, the Scripture does not indicate to me that the dead in Christ have this freedom. The account of Lazarus and the rich man tell me there is a great gulf fixed between Heaven and Hell, it tells me that "one from the dead" (lost) cannot come back to earth. But it tells me more!

The angels of God were sent to escort Lazarus into paradise! However, this man did not go to paradise, he did not die! I will use the chaplain's words, "I really don't know how to explain it." Would angels appear to frighten a dying man? Of course not! The angels of God would appear to comfort a dear saint, to assure him. The man was fully aware of every word spoken, every movement and action taken in the room while he was "clinically dead." I believe God allowed this man a glimpse of glory. My personal opinion in this given situation is that two angels took on a recognizable form and ministered to this dying saint who did not die. There are numerous accounts of similar visions in time of death and danger. Now let me be quick to say, Satan would have you clinically analyze this and call it hallucination! Let me urge you to spiritually and scripturally examine such experiences, and this is not contrary to Scripture. Stephen, while dying, spoke "I see Jesus..." (Acts 7:55-60).

Stories of dying lost men are just as numerous, but the opposite is true in their release from this life. One hospital spokesman told me of cries of "No, someone help me!" "Don't let me leave this body." Some have described visions of snakes and spiders. Does Satan send his mongrels for the unbelievers? "The rich man died, and was buried and ...in Hell..." (Luke 16:22-23).

It is clear that the angels of God are not visibly sent to everyone. Angelic activity increased as the birth of Jesus neared. This is true because millions and millions of believers have never seen or heard an angel. This does nothing to disprove their ministry, nor does it discredit God's Word. It is a reflection upon man's complete faith in the Supernatural God. There is no activity of God apart from His Spirit. "For God is a Spirit and they that worship Him must worship Him in Spirit and truth" (John 4:24).

The Holy angels are a part of God's Holy Creation; man is a part of His Redemptive Creation, and faith joins the two. Just as man believes in God by faith, as he accepts His word by faith, he accepts the reality of angels by faith.

Unholy man is joined to our Holy God by the redemptive work of Jesus. As the Redeemed of God and an heir of salvation, I have Holy angels ministering for me. Not because I am Holy, but because He is Holy and I am His. Let me repeat again, there are many things that angels are not, but they are not gone! The liberal, or the slow in faith, might call Heavenly revelation, hallucination. He hurts himself! Bible wisdom and spiritual discernment are imperative as we experience the supernatural.

God's angels are alive and well, working in the lives of believers. Don't be slow to believe. Be scripturally sound, and don't be surprised when God's angels move about you. Billy Graham asks this question in his book, *Angels: God's Secret Agents,* "Have you ever seen an angel?" I would ask further, would you *like* to see an angel?

I have posed this question to many Christians. Many said, "No"; a handful said, "Yes." Though it is not necessary to my faith, I would like to see one of God's Holy Messengers.

The angels are not gone! Perhaps this is an inconclusive statement. If they are not gone, where are they? Remember, angels are spirits; they are not visible to the human eye. However, angels are not limited to just an "invisible spiritual existence." If God so chooses, an angel can appear in a form recognizable to man. Human eyes do not often perceive the presence of angels, in the majority of cases. As ministering spirits, (Hebrews 1: 14), they are not visible. The exception is rare, extremely rare, in our daily work. You can talk with thousands of Christians and never meet one who has seen an angel.

Let us look further at what angels are not. Compared with believers, there are few similarities. The angels cannot call God "Father" as a believer does, for we know God the Father through redemption. We have sinned; the Holy angels have not, and have no need of salvation. Jesus did not die for the angels. They know God as their Creator and Master, but not as God who gave His only begotten Son for them.

The angels are not filled or indwelt by the Holy Spirit; again the distinction is made by relationship to God. The Holy Spirit is given to believers only. Since the angels are not "born again," they are not indwelt with the Holy Spirit. However, they are subject to the Spirit's direction in that the Holy Spirit is God in the Third Person.

The angels are not heirs of God, nor heirs of salvation. They are not joint-heirs with Jesus Christ. The angels are not going to share in our inheritance. Heaven comes to the believer, again, because of redemption. Angels have not had this experience. Furthermore, they *cannot* have this experience. The angels cannot even bear personal witness of salvation. The privilege of sharing Jesus' redemptive death and resurrection is denied to the angels. They can rejoice at His Coming, at His Resurrection, His Ascension and Return, but they have to remain silent at Calvary. They can rejoice when man receives Jesus, but angels cannot bear personal witness of salvation by experience.

Angels are not confined to heaven and earth. This earth is not the only place inhabited by angels. Out there in the vastness of infinity, beyond the comprehension of the human mind, beyond our ability to grasp, there are nevertheless ministering spirits called the angels of God.

Jesus said, "Likewise, I say unto you, there is joy in the presence of angels of God over one sinner that repenteth," (Luke 15:10). They are everywhere and in close contact with the events of heaven and earth. Angels are in heaven worshiping and praising God, and just as surely angels are ministering for the saints here on earth. Remember they are not ministering to us but **for** us!

Much more could be written about what angels are not, but the greatest truth I can leave you with is that they most certainly are not gone!

Chapter 3

MANUFACTURER'S MARK

Colossians 1:6 *For by Him were all things created, that are in heaven, and that are in earth, visible and invisible, whether they be thrones, or dominions, or principalities, or powers: all things were created by Him, and for Him.*

Possibly the clearest truth we can draw from all angelic study is that they are created beings created by God Himself, through the Lord Jesus Christ. Scripture leaves no doubt about the angels' Creator: "All things were made by Him: and without Him was not any thing made that was made" (John 1:3).

This is one point in "angelology" that finds full agreement with denominational scholars. Yet there is a shroud of mysticism even about the angels beginning. God's Word reveals to man only what God wants man to know about Him and there is *no revelation* apart from God's Word. If you believe the Bible, you will believe in the ministry of angels. You will believe the angels were created by God. However, little is said about the angels prior to man's creation. Through Bible study and scriptural genealogies man has come to a general conclusion as to the age of man. According to Dr. C. I. Scofield, he is dated from 4-6 thousand years B.C. Although man's beginning is an interesting study and worthy of attention, let it suffice at this point to say there is not a hint in Scripture as to the age of angels. God, in His Sovereignty, did not choose to reveal much of heaven's happenings prior to man's existence. Ezekiel 28 and Isaiah 14 tell something of angels before their fall. It is clear that the angels of God were made by the Master.

The Scripture puts God's mark upon all creation and angels are included. Man poses many questions that are foolish and insignificant to those who "walk by faith." It seems to be in our nature to ask when, why, and what. But, I cannot find answers in Scripture to all of these questions about angels. To speculate is often unwise. There was a time in church history when the topic of angels was of such interest that men argued over how many angels could dance upon the head of a pin. Ridiculous as that may seem, Satan succeeded in pushing angels and their ministry from the teaching and preaching of their ministry from the church. So much was said concerning angels in the middle centuries that Christians were worshiping and praying to them, such as the Catholic-introduced "patron saints." The doctrine of angels was preached and taught by some to the extent of neglecting Jesus and the heart of the Gospel. Rather than coming back to the central truth of the Gospel of Jesus Christ, and giving angels their proper place in the Scriptures, angels were soon omitted. Pulpits have been remarkably silent for centuries. As is the case so often, the pendulum swings right and left, passing by the middle with each swing. Jesus is the heart of the Gospel, but let us not forget that the angels are His, and to know Him also means that His angels minister to us.

Satan is making a bid today, with some success, to blind the church to the supernatural activity about us in the form of demons and angels. Be honest with yourself now; have you been prone to attribute all things that you don't understand to Satan? I believe this is dangerous. First of all, Satan is not an all-encompassing spirit as is Jehovah God. To blame him is scripturally inaccurate as he can only be in one place at any given time. It is his underlings, the demons, with whom we battle.

I believe even more dangerous are those who do not understand spiritual gifts and fear them so much that they make foolish statements such as, "That could be of the Devil." It seems that many times that gifts of the Spirit are often rationalized with this kind of thinking. I believe it is borderline blasphemy. Now, before you react too quickly to that statement, let me say this: understanding an "experience" is not a sufficient basis for judgement. Our convictions must be based on scriptural understanding. God will not work apart from Scripture!

The opposite extreme is to desire a feeling, experience or sign, in order to try God. Unusual, supernatural experiences are not necessary to the Christian faith. *But neither are they to be avoided.* If God wants to take you deeper into His grace and love, follow Him by faith in His Word. Angels are active today! They are active in the lives of believers.

But what about unbelievers, and what about fallen angels? Somewhere in God's history nothing existed but God, Triune God. I cannot give you an exact sequence of active events, but I can tell you angels were created before man.

A host of questions have come my way concerning angels and many, many times my answer was simply, "I don't know." Saying "I don't know" does not bother me when no one else knows either.

I believe speculation should have reasonable scriptural support, so I will speak about what I believe to be true. Angels were created by God and were created before man. And the exact time of their creation cannot be dated

What did God create when He created angels? Here, I have scriptural help and can speak with a degree of confidence. Lucifer was created, along with an untold number of angelic beings. It is clear that not all angels were created equal in the true sense of that statement. They were created with various degrees of power, rank, and responsibility. Three angels are mentioned by name in the King James Bible (the Catholic version mentions a fourth, Raphael, in the book of Tibeus).

I am totally satisfied with God's revelation through the King James Bible. Lucifer, Michael, and Gabriel are mentioned by name. They qualify according to Scripture as the most prominent of the multitudes created. They are referred to as archangels.

The church has been unsettled on the question of angels. At one point in history, it was common belief that there were seven archangels. This view was adopted largely because the number 7 is symbolically God's perfect number. It is His number of perfection and completion. It is quite possible that this is true, but the Bible does not say so.

Later scholars decided there were four archangels, Michael, Gabriel, Lucifer, and "Raphael." Much of early church history is recorded by the Catholic Church. This is conjecture and not supported by Scripture. Billy Graham states in his book, *Angels: God's Secret Agents,* that he believes there were two archangels, Lucifer and Michael. Since we will discuss this later let me just say there is no way of absolutely knowing. God's Word is our only source of belief. Lucifer, regardless of his original state, is now known as Satan and has been kicked out of heaven. He is now referred to in Scripture as the 'god of this world.'

The question here is not when angels were created, but when and how did they fall? Did Lucifer, in his rebellion, fall before man was created? Was he here before the Genesis account of creation and responsible for the "gap theory" between Genesis 1:1 and 1:2? Did his fall cause the chaotic condition on earth prior to God's creation of man on the sixth day?

If there was no other account of angels than that of the fallen angels, we could conclude they have (had) the freedom of choice (Jude 6). They also have emotion (Ezek. 28:12-17). The infamous 5 "I wills" of Lucifer indicate that he was proud of being an "angel of light." Isaiah 14:12-14 gives us an indication that the reason for Lucifer's fall may give a hint as to when he fell. (Read the six "I wills" of God in Ezekiel as a response to Satan's proud boast). Some have suggested that Lucifer's pride was also created in God's image. He created man with a living soul, and a capacity to love his Creator voluntarily. Some believe the rebellion and fall came immediately after the creation of Adam and Eve. I believe, however, that Satan was already here when man was created and had been reduced to being the "god of this world." He was kicked out of heaven and Jesus said in Luke 10:18, "I beheld Satan as lightening fall from heaven." Jesus saw it because He likely is the One who booted Satan to the ground. The Bible simply does not say when this happened.

This war will continue as Lucifer, "the star of the morning," and his host of followers futilely fight against God and God's people. His doom is sealed and revealed to us in the Book of Revelation. Angels are sometimes referred to as "stars"; Lucifer was. In the book of Revelation, John mentions a third of the stars being swept from heaven to the earth (Rev. 12:4, paraphrased). These fallen creatures now torment mankind in a futile attempt to "get back at God." We know them as demon powers. Once they praised Jehovah God, now they blaspheme Him and have, along with their fallen master, come to steal, kill and destroy.

Paul warns the believer that our battles are spiritual battles, fought against "spiritual wickedness in high places." He calls Satan "the prince and power of the air–the ruler of darkness." Although the Proverbs deal with "man's pride," there is an insight to Satan's fall. One of the seven things God hates is a "proud look." Lucifer, as many have pointed out, was full of pride. As Jesus talked of the rich man who said, "I will, I will..." etc., He said of this man, "Thou fool, this night shall thy soul be required of thee," "I will" are the words of a fool when God is left out. When our will becomes submissive to His will, the words can become those of a Moses or a Paul, "I will..." follow Jesus. "I will...do what He wants me to do" are words of victory for the believer.

The Apostle Paul asked the Lord, "What will thou have me to do?" These words must sound sweet to Our Lord when we in love say to Him, "Lord, show me what to do and I will." However, Lucifer's "I will" was in defiance of God. He was not satisfied as a radiant angel of light, the star of the morning. He was called the anointed cherub, but he wanted more. In Isaiah 14:13-14 Satan made five boastful statements, leading to his being cast down to the earth.

1. "I will ascend into heaven..."
2. "I will exalt my throne above the stars of God..."
3. "I will sit also on the mount of the congregation..."
4. "I will ascend above the heights of the clouds..."
5. "I will be like the most high."

Can the creature ascend above the Creator? Lucifer, for all of his brilliance, position with God, and super-natural intelligence, appears as a fool in thinking he could ascend above God! Satan's or Lucifer's sin has become the basic sin of the universe. Read that statement again.

In every case of personal witnessing that I can recall, man's excuse for not trusting Jesus was the sin of pride! It was this approach that the fallen angel took toward Eve "... eat and be like God." Let me inject this thought here. What Lucifer did was stupid, and it was foolish. But it was bold! It was reckless! He is dangerous and deceitful! Peter describes him as a "roaring lion... seeking whom he may devour." I simply say to that, "Well, he best look somewhere else because he MAY NOT devour me!" Certainly God's people can be demonized, but not possessed, or as Dr. Charles Stanley says, they cannot be totally possessed. Believers can have oppression from demon spirits in the body or soul but not in the spirit. The spirit is the dwelling place of God's Holy Spirit. The spirit is willing but the flesh . . . the flesh, the body and soul are weak. The soul is comprised of our mind, will and emotions, if demon spirits oppress believers it must be in those areas and then only by permission. (See our books on demons and deliverance, *SERPENTS IN THE SANCTUARY* and *TURMOIL IN THE TEMPLE.*)

Child of God be careful, but not frightened! Satan can only touch believers with God's permission, or the consent of the individual by opening doorways to the evil ones. God's Holy angels stand all about us. Though a perpetual war be raging all about us, God's angels are just awaiting the call to claim victory. The mark of the manufacturer is on Lucifer in that he was free-willed. The fact that he was "made by the master" makes him subject to the Master. One of God's great evangelists remarked, "Satan is on a leash and God is holding the leash!" Demon powers must have "legal" permission to enter the soul or flesh of a believer.

Is Lucifer's power limited? Job, chapters 1 and 2, tell of his power over the elements. He is not omnipotent, but he has awesome powers (see, Isaiah 13:12-24). He uses his power to create havoc on earth, powers of fire, flood, earthquake, storm, disease, influencing moral corruption and the downfall of nations. Still, Christian, do not despair, he is subject to God in all areas. He cannot move except as God allows it.

God and His Holy angels could at any time move to stop his onslaught. Scripture tells me at the appointed time He will, and *one,* just *one,* of God's angelic host will bind Lucifer and cast him into a bottomless pit.

This is not to imply that God is ultimately responsible for all evil. Rather God's graciousness caused Him to create the angels as well as man with the ability to choose. We could have been robots. My point here is that we be aware of the cunning devices of the fallen angels. The Scripture declares that God "sent" a messenger of Satan to "buffet" Paul. God provided all the grace Paul needed. Holy angels stood ready to minister to Paul's needs.

Witchcraft, demons, astrology (falsely called science), Satan worship, and such, are just a few of the signs of the fallen angels working today. Mental illness, depression, family dysfunction, fears, corruption and other oppressive deeds are the work of the demon powers. The emergency rooms, the cemeteries, the crippled and maimed, the lingering stench of war; disease, hatred, bloodshed are all about us. All stand as evidence of the fallen angels and the results of sin, of transgressing God's Holy Law, of refusing the sweet Lord Jesus as Savior.

Jesus went about doing good and healing all those who were oppressed of the devil, (Acts 10:38), and He still is!

The one who knows best about Satan's evil spirit world wrote the best book that I have ever found on the subject. I highly recommend it for all mankind. It is, of course, the Bible. Although it is necessary in a study of angels to include the fallen angels, my purpose for writing is to manifest God's angelic host, to cause faith and confidence to abound in the lives of believers.

What I have said about fallen angels was said as a warning to non-believers and as a spiritual insight to believers. No fallen angel has ever been able to stand and proclaim *"All power is given unto me. . .in heaven and in earth."* The Lord Jesus made this statement and He is their Creator. At the name of Jesus Christ fallen angels must also bow.

The demons in the man from Gadara, named Legion, possessed of many spirits of the evil world, could do nothing but ask for mercy when Jesus came, (Mark 5). The fallen angels know they cannot abide when the legal rights are canceled and Jesus commands them to leave. The born again believer can rejoice, for with his salvation came Holy angels to minister and they bear the manufacturer's mark, made in heaven by Jesus!

Chapter 4

MINISTRY TO MEN

Hebrews 1: 14 *"Are they not all ministering spirits sent forth to minister for them who shall be heirs of salvation."*

There are almost 300 mentions of angels in Scripture. References to Holy angels far outnumber the mention of fallen angels or demons. However, there are few mentions of any of the "angels' dealings that are not directly related to man.

Angels are referred to 273 times in Scripture: 108 times in the Old Testament and 165 times in the New Testament. The cherubim are mentioned 21 times in one chapter, the seraphim only in Isaiah, chapter 6. As matter of interest only, angels are referred to at least an average of 4 times per book in the Bible.

My reason, again, for mentioning this is that, in almost every case, the angels are somehow connected with man. Recently, just in the past few years, there has been much talk about the Holy Spirit, about gifts of the spirit, tongues, prophecies, "second blessing," baptism in the spirit, and there has been much confusion and division as a result.

But, please note, disagreement does not necessarily produce disunity. A lack of forgiveness does! A lack of compassion and understanding does. The term "Charismatic" has become frightening to some believers and almost sacred to others. Let me be quick to say that this study in angels has nothing to do with either group of believers. If you are born again you are subject to the ministry of angels.

I suppose it would be good to draw a spiritual line to distinguish between the ministry of God's Holy Spirit and God's Holy angels. Their ministries are separate and distinct; most scholars agree that Bible doctrine in this area is clear:

(1) The Holy Spirit ministers TO our spiritual needs; comforts, leads, guides, directs into all truth.

(2) The Holy angels minister FOR us, often involving the physical needs of believers. Daniel in the lion's den, Peter in prison, etc.

I believe more needs to be said. We are talking about Holy activity. Nothing can be done apart from God the Father, God the Son, and God the Holy Spirit. Angels are Holy "spirits" and move as directed by Holy Dictate. In this sense their ministries should not be separated, instead, they give us a glimpse of God's Holy provisions for believers, that is, Holy Deity directs them!

The Scripture gives no answer as to why angels appear to some and not to others. There seems to be no pattern for when and how God's Holy angels make themselves visible to men. Would you like to see an angel? When my children were younger I recall asking this question of my 10-year-old son. He thought for a moment and said, "Yes sir, I would, but I think it would scare me." My 7-year-old son immediately replied, "God's angels don't scare you, they make you feel happy."

I have asked the same question of many believers, most said yes, and they also believed it would be a frightening experience. Those who said they did not want to see an angel fall pretty much in the category of those who don't care to see anything of God.

Think of the "things" in your presence right now that you cannot see and cannot hear. You are not even aware of the presence of radio signals, hundreds passing by your ears just now. Unless you have a receiver you cannot know what is being broadcast. Television pictures beam 'round about you; without a receiver you will not see them, they are not visible to the human eye, but they are there. You have, no doubt, sat in your home and watched men walk on God's moon, you even heard them speak.

The space center in Houston says this is possible not because of a powerful transmitter, but a powerful receiver. The receiver is the key to successful transmission. I believe that is also true of Holy communication with God.
As difficult as it is for our minds to grasp all that goes on about us, even an unbelieving scientist would admit that space travel, transmitting and receiving audio and video, etc., has not even scratched the surface of God's universe. Scientist now believe there may be as many as 250 billion galaxies like ours. I'm thinking it is more like 247 billion. I mean we are guessing at this point, aren't we?

Light from earth reaches the moon in 1 and 1/3 seconds. The moon is 240,000 miles from our earth and man reached it after 6 thousand years of compiling knowledge and of discovering God's laws. God sends the light at the rate of 186,000 miles per second and He simply said, "Let there be light." He speaks and the entire universe obeys. Now with this in mind let me ask again, would you like to see an angel?

I have never seen an angel, but this does nothing to weaken my faith in God's Holy throng. I believe that angels may travel from the presence of God to minister to man in a flash! Do they move faster than the speed of light? I don't know. I do know that as God directs, they move to minister to man. I would like to see an angel. I would like all that God can give to me and trust me with; I am not shy in receiving what God wants me to have. But I have not seen an angel.

Old Testament saints saw angels, and angels are mentioned as early as Genesis 3:24, just 80 verses deep into God's great book. Abraham saw and conversed with angels; the men of Sodom and Gomorrah, "unbelievers," saw two angels (though they recognized them only as men). Moses, Balaam, and other Old Testament characters to be discussed later, also saw angels.

Angels ministered unto the Lord Jesus in His bodily form. Paul, Peter, and John are examples that we will also discuss later. There is no question among Bible scholars, both liberal and conservative, that angels were active in "Biblical days," the real question seems to be in the NOW. The absence of miraculous testimonies about the angels leaves question to some as to whether or not their ministry is valid.

Are angels active today?

Yes, it is even possible to be in the presence of a visible angelic being and be "unaware" of it. "Be not forgetful to entertain strangers: for thereby some have entertained angels unawares" (Hebrews 13:2). How could this be? Is this verse just to mean that some Old Testament prophets did so? Hardly. It is written to believers and indicates that angels obviously do one of two things, or both:

(1) They appear as ordinary men and would give us no indication they were God sent.

(2) They are about us always, invisible and we are not aware of their presence.

I personally believe they do both! As is the case so often in studying the supernatural, information comes second-hand. I will relate some "second-hand" experiences now. I have been told by numerous sound-minded, scripturally-accurate believers, of angelic visitors. Renowned gospel singer, Francine Morrison, told me of "seeing the backside of an angel." I sat in the living room of this dear saint of God who sings internationally for Jesus. She told of praying for God to send angels to watch over her home, at every window and one at every door. She lives in a humble home in the high crime area of Fort Worth. Because of her frequent travels, she felt her home was especially vulnerable to thieves. At one point in her life, after praying for God's angelic protection, she had thoughts of having metal bars installed over her windows and doors. She related to me that one night it "seemed" as though God was speaking to her very softly, "If you put up the bars, I will remove my angels." She told me as she prayed to thank the Lord for this assurance her doorbell rang. She went to the door. "I looked through this little peephole," she said as she pointed to the door, "but I could not see anyone." She opened the door and said she saw standing, with arms folded and his back to the door, one of God's Holy angels. His brightness was such that, "I believe I would have died if I had seen his face."

The glory of God was so magnificent she was awestruck. She described the heavenly creature to me. He was very large, larger than a man; he had two large beautiful wings and was dressed more as a "Roman soldier" than anything else she could describe. The angel in his physical, or visible, form did not stay long, just long enough to assure her (in her words) that "God had His angels all about her and she need not worry about her home, while at home or on the road."

There is more. Soon after this experience she was in another town, in another part of the country, singing her songs about Jesus. A burglar went into her home. Did the angels fail? They cannot fail! The burglar was unable to take anything. A neighbor was awakened (by an 'angel'?) for some reason and called the police, suspecting something was wrong. Her husband, who was at work, for "some reason" felt he must go home. Police arrived, her husband arrived, the burglar, empty-handed, walked out the driveway side door into the waiting hands of Fort Worth police officers. Her husband was there to verify nothing was missing and to press charges. Were God's angels at work? Were they on the job in response to the prayer (to God) of "an heir" of salvation? Recall the words of the angel Gabriel as he appeared to Zacharias in the temple, "fear not, Zacharias; for thy prayer is heard". . . and "I am sent (from God) to speak unto thee. . ." (Luke 1:13,19).

Every account I have received from believers I have checked out against God's Word. I have found nothing contrary to Scripture. My faith has only been strengthened by numerous testimonies of God's children being ministered for by angels.

A teenage Christian told me of a glorious feeling that came over him while in the mountains of Colorado. He had been seeking a deeper relationship with the Lord. He told me he spent much time just walking in the woods, praising God and meditating on His great love. He had become an astute student of the Scripture, he read it and loved every word of it. He said he simply could not get enough of sensing God's sweet presence.

While there in Colorado, almost a recluse, he wrote music to God's glory and sang just to the Creator and His Creation. One evening he said he felt unusually close to the Lord. Some of his friends were inside, some singing and reading God's Word. While, outside the cabin, he was just basking in the glory of God's love and listening to that "still small voice." He told me of hearing the most beautiful voice, singing praise to God. He said he was so excited about this "heavenly singing" that he ran into the cabin and asked if they were singing. Had they heard the music, the voice? They had not, but did not doubt that he had. Did an angel visit this young believer? There was no message given, but he said, "There was an assurance in my heart, I knew God had visited with me somehow." He said, "I believe God sent an angel, I believe it with all my heart!"

A pastor friend of mine, Rev. Ernest McGee, has related several instances of heavenly visitors. Is God selective to those who have "experiences" that you and I have not had? Every decision God makes is wise and rational, not merely arbitrary.

"Whatever God wants to do is all right with me." I can honestly say that is my prayer to God. I do not know what one does to receive heavenly visions; desiring them in a sense is dangerous, if the believer is not able to discern the spirits. Yet, a genuine desire to be close to God must be a prerequisite. Let me say this about "my pastor friend" before I relate some of his dealings with the heavenly. He is not "Charismatic"; he is not "Pentecostal"; he is not a "holy roller"... as some would say. This pastor is not part of a "splinter group," he is a Baptist and avid student of the Scripture. I don't think I have known anyone who loves God's Word as does this man.

He has had numerous visits by angelic beings. He said, "They always bring a message from God, but never in conflict with Scripture. Sometimes, it is just to make me know that God's hand is upon me. Sometimes," he says, "they bring messages of warning."

I asked this preacher if he was ever frightened or alarmed when these visions suddenly appeared. "Oh, no," he said, "No, no, you are so caught up in the glory of the vision or visitation of an angel that you do not think of fear. The only regret of these visits is that when they are over, you wish it could have lasted longer. You wonder why you could not keep the presence of the heavenly messenger. You feel so much of God that you don't want to let go." But he says, "They visit briefly, they bring their message and then they are gone. They may not appear again for months, or years, but when God sends His messengers you always know it is of God."

This same pastor has had much tribulation in his life. I could safely compare him with a modern day Job. He is the closest of any man I have ever met or known of in my lifetime to compare with the Biblical Job. Several years ago, he and his wife discovered their son had leukemia. He had several other children, so you may take this lightly. I hope not! While his son was suffering with this disease, a multitude of problems began to creep into his life. He was in a terrible car accident while going to preach a funeral. He was disabled and could not work. The church offering alone could not meet the building payments. Personal bills, doctor's bills, began to mount. He faced foreclosure on his home and church, for the salary he received from working was supplementing the small church offering as well as his house payments. During the two years his son struggled with leukemia, this man had a heart attack and was told by his doctors that he could not preach. "It seemed," he said, "at times that God had completely turned His back on me. But," he added, "I knew that was not true."

He told me of how the angels visited his son in the hospital on numerous occasions. He told of how refreshing it was to him to hear his dying son describe how beautiful the

45

"heavenly beings" were, how he talked of speaking with and listening to the angels of God. From age 11 until age 14 this child related scripturally sound experiences with God's Holy angels. I visited this boy many times and talked with him. He told me his favorite verse of Scripture was John 11:25,26, "...he that believeth in me, though he were dead, yet shall he live; and whosoever liveth and believeth in me shall never die..."

It was in the moments that he meditated on the sweet promises, that the angels of God would visit with him and assure him of heaven.

A few days before God sent his Holy angels to escort this young saint home, I visited with him in the Intensive Care ward. As I talked to him about Jesus he smiled. His body was swollen and puffy, the signs of death were evident but he smiled at Jesus' name. He could not speak because of a tube in his throat; he lifted up his left wrist and turned it so I could see. He had scratched into his arm a scar that went with him to his grave. On his wrist he carved, "I hate the Devil."

His father told me that the angels of God had come in and manifested to him as an answer to the child's prayer. He had asked the Lord why he was suffering. Angels told him the Devil (Lucifer) had been allowed to touch his body but also gave him sweet assurance that he was going to a better place. The child told me just a few days before he died how anxious he was to be with Jesus.

I love these kinds of testimonies! It strengthens my faith in Scripture and the promise that angels are, "...all ministering spirits, sent forth to minister for them who shall be heirs of salvation."

The boy died at approximately 8:15 a.m. on a Sunday morning. His father was up all night with the child. He felt the final jerk of death as he pulled his son to his bosom; he laid the child back on the hospital bed. He was dead! That pastor called me moments later to give me the news. I asked if he would like for me to preach for him that day, feeling the remorse of his soul. "No," he said, "Don, I believe the thing I could do now to best please the Master is to go to His sacred pulpit and preach the unsearchable riches of Christ." Just prior to his son's last breath, God had given the struggling, suffering preacher a heavenly glimpse and bathed him in his grace and love. Grace sufficient! I will share the details of his "heavenly glimpse" later. Words I want to share now are a result of God's "ministering spirits" and God's Holy Spirit.

"Don," he said, "If they throw me in the streets and cut off my head, my last words will be, 'Jesus lives.'"

Take courage, child of God, He will meet your every need. All of heaven moves at His command!

Chapter 5

MULTITUDES AND MIGHTY

Rev. 5:11 *And I beheld, and heard the voice of many angels round about the throne and the beasts and the elders; and the number of them was ten thousand times ten thousand, and thousands of thousands.*

Did you ever wonder how many angels God created? Down through Church history there has been much speculation about this, but that's all it is, just speculation. Concerning the number of angels created, again, we can only draw from what Scripture reveals to us. However, it is safe to assume that if the number of angels could be known, it would be mind-boggling. Our "finite" shrinks in understanding as we grope with the Infinite Mind of God. I would not want to serve a God small enough for me to understand, for then He would be too small to take care of my problems. The vastness of God's angelic host should bring humility to the proudest of human hearts.

The Book of Psalms, in many places, declares the glory of God's heavens. Psalm 19:1 states, "The heavens declare the glory of God; and the firmament sheweth his handiwork." It staggers the imagination to look into the heavens and try to grasp the size of the universe. In my lifetime, I have touched the lives of those who knew only the horse and buggy as the best means of transportation. My great-grandparents would tell of moving about by basically the same means of transportation as man had four to six thousand years ago. Not so much progress for such a length of time. Yet, in contrast, my two children have lived in an age that has now known space travel. To them, men going to the moon are commonplace. My life has seen tremendous progress; from the horse and buggy to space age in just a few short years. Amazing? Yes, and no! Our world seems so large when we think in terms of property, population, travel, etc., yet it seems so small, so tiny, when we are reminded by scientists that our dwelling place is but a "Speck of Dust" in God's vast creation.

Our nearest celestial neighbor is the moon, some 240,000 miles away. Our next closest neighbor is Mars, and it is thirty-seven million miles away. If it were possible for man to visit Mars and look back to the earth, scientists say it would appear as a mere star. My child-like mind still wants to think of the stars as small glittering lights in the heavens, but I am told that 25 billion miles from our earth every star is a shining sun.

Think briefly on this, if you could cruise at a non-stop speed of 40 miles per hour (some bicycles travel that fast now), you would remain at this cruising speed for 75 million years before arriving at the nearest star. Then, 60 billion miles away, there are more stars and suns. My mind cannot think in such deep channels. What is beyond that? If space has an end...what is on the other side? Man is a fool...to play with the Mind of God! I believe God's Word records it best: David, the Psalmist, said, "When I consider the heavens, the work of thy fingers, the moon and the stars that thou has ordained; what is man that thou art mindful of him?" (Psalm 8:3,4). God's creation is so vast, so immense! What all is out there?

Are there living creatures like man somewhere other than just on "our" little globe? Would God have such a vast universe and have only one little ball inhabited with life? Man's curiosity leads him to search the heavens; our findings, though marvelous in achievement, find no evidence of life. Do angels fit in this discussion? Do they perhaps play an unseen role in all of God's handiwork?

When the Apostle Paul speaks of a "third heaven," to what does he refer? With this question in mind, let's recall that man is "created a little lower than the angels..." Could it be that the angels of God are the tenants of the heavens? If this is true, there is of necessity a need for many, mighty angelic beings! Hebrews 12:22 makes mention of "an innumerable company of angels." The writer makes no attempt to number them; rather, he says they cannot be numbered! Again, David says in the Psalms, "The chariots of God are twenty thousand, even thousands of angels: the Lord is among them ..." (Psalm 68:17).

It is clear just from the few Scripture references given that the vastness of God's creation includes a vast number of angels. A sweet truth we can glean from the previous Scripture is that "The Lord is among them." I am excited about the number of angels that the Lord has created.

I am happy to know that the Lord is among them!

Man's interest in angels is evidenced in the popularity of such books as *The Chariots of The Gods*. The thought of ancient astronauts has generated much interest. Our study has nothing to do with speculation or theory. Rather, it has to do with the fact of God's Holy angels. The angels are Holy because the Lord is among them. This truth will not change. "When the Lord Jesus shall be revealed from heaven with His mighty angels" (II Thess. 1:7). Plural phrases such as this only indicate that there are many, mighty angels. The obvious is not to attempt to calculate the number of angels, but to realize they are "innumerable."

I get the feeling that this is what Billy Graham was thinking when he wrote, Angels: *God's Secret Agents* The thought makes me rejoice. We are surrounded by God's Holy angels. I am convinced of at least two things at this point:

(1) There is no place that man could go and escape God's Presence. Remember, "The Lord is among them..."

(2) The angels of God are present wherever God is.

Let me be quick to say that God is Omnipresent! No single angel is; they are present because of God, they are His.

No scriptural study will ever reveal the number of angels. However, the more one studies god's angels, the more he becomes pleasantly aware of the untold millions that move at His command. At least 66 times in the Bible's 66th book, angels are mentioned actively carrying out God's marvelous plan. An army of angels is mentioned fighting under the command of the archangel, Michael. For centuries men have wondered, is there "intelligent life" on other planets. Almost with tongue in cheek, the answer is yes; scriptural truth declares the angels are there and to be sure they are "intelligent life." They are alive, intelligent, but invisible to the human eye.

One Christmas morning, my two sons received a pair of "walkie-talkies" as gifts. Until those little sets were turned on, I was not aware that there were so many voices going through my home. I had not heard them before and I am quite certain they did not come the same day the "walkie-talkies" came. The little receivers were picking up voices from all over the neighborhood, all over the city; the voices of men and women I did not know came into my home. What had changed? Nothing had changed, but something heretofore unheard was now being heard. Hundreds of strange voices in my home and I was not conscious of it. All that had changed was a little receiver now in my home, sensitive to sound frequencies. This little receiver opened my mind to a much greater truth. Not hearing the voices did not change the fact of their existence. Hearing the voices did not make the fact a greater truth. It does lead me to make one simple statement: because you have not seen angelic beings is not a good reason to doubt their existence. They are in the air, everywhere.

We have now come to a dividing line even among fundamental Bible believers. Are angels active today, NOW? Some make bold dogmatic statements; others shy away from even an opinion. I will be cautious here, not to present a dogma, but an opinion. A. C. Gaebelein, stated: "The heavens are silent. Angels are no longer seen for the reason that God expects man to believe in His completed revelation."

Further, he states, "There is Scripture evidence which makes this clear." However, he gives no Scripture evidence to support his statement. He mentions also, "There are also many traditions and legends from earliest times which claim that holy men and women were visited by angels. But no one can vouch for the genuineness of these things."

I believe this is ridiculous thinking. No one can vouch for Jesus coming into my life and redeeming me either. "Vouching" is contrary to faith and all Biblical principles!

He says very clearly that he does not believe that angels visibly appear to men NOW, and he gives two reasons:

>1) God expects man to believe in His completed revelation.
>2) No one can vouch for the genuineness of angelic appearances.

I personally believe God does permit some angelic visions. Believing in His completed revelation, the Bible did not prevent Heavenly messengers appearing to man Heb. 13:2). It is no more necessary to have someone vouch, for angelic appearances than for someone to vouch for an individual's salvation experience. I will give further reasons for believing this later. Let me say here, don't limit God's moving in your life because you have not known Him to move thus in another's. Your only checkpoint must be God's Word. His Holy angels have no message or working apart from it.

Theologians down through the ages have divided angels into categories or divisions of rank and authority. As I study

God's Word about angels, I can see clearly there are divisions of rank and power. Some scholars have them in divisions of nine or ten categories. I don't like to overwork a statement, but the Bible is just not clear in this area. The many mentions of angels and their various roles in the Book of Revelation tells me that any list of rank or power would be inadequate. Generally angelic study reveals a list similar to this:

1. Archangels
2. Angels
3. Seraphim
4. Cherubim
5. Principalities
6. Authorities
7. Might
8. Power
9. Thrones
10. Dominion

Looking closely at Colossians 1:16 would give me space to believe this may very well be a list of celestial creatures. A glance at Paul's warning to Christians in Ephesians 6:12 tells me further this category would include fallen angels: "For we wrestle not against flesh and blood, but against principalities, against powers, against the rulers of the darkness of this world, against spiritual wickedness in high places." Certainly, it is clear here that principalities and powers are a part of Lucifer's domain also.

Romans 8:38,39 also lends weight to angelic categories; "nor angels, nor principalities, nor powers... shall be able to separate us from the love of God, which is in Christ

Jesus our Lord." My point is that "principalities ... powers," may or may not be angelic. I personally believe they are, but I will speak where the Bible is clear and list five divisions of rank or celestial organization:

1. Archangels
2. Special Messengers
3. Cherubim
4. Seraphim
5. Guardians.

Earlier I mentioned that throughout church history there has been disagreement on the number of archangels. Some, for no apparent scriptural reason, chose to believe that originally there were seven archangels. The only speck of support I can see here is that God's number of completion and perfection throughout His word is the number seven. However, there is a problem here, for if there were seven, six of them lost their position, for only one is mentioned in Scripture. Some say there were four: Michael, Gabriel, Lucifer, and Raphael (Raphael is mentioned in the Catholic Bible). Others seem satisfied that there were originally three: Michael, Gabriel, and Lucifer. There are at least two other views. One is that, originally, Michael and Lucifer were archangels. Lucifer's obvious power and strength in waging war in the heavens is good reason for believing this and I really have no problem with this theological view.

I personally believe there were three archangels. Lucifer appeared to be in charge of praise and worship in heaven and was likely over 1/3 of the angels. That's how many he took with him in his foolish rebellion and ultimate banishment from God's Presence. The other two thirds I believe are now under the leadership of Michael and Gabriel. It would seem that Michael is the strongest of angels and heads up the warring angels. Gabriel, then, would be over the remaining 1/3 of messenger angels.

My real question would be, did Lucifer lose any of his power when he fell? I don't know if he did, Scripture does "indicate" that he was an archangel. In Revelation 20:1-3 God's word says one angel will..."from heaven lay hold on Satan and bind him." That one angel will likely be Michael.

The only mention of the archangel is in Jude, v. 9, "yet Michael the archangel..." Regardless of what was, Michael, now, is the archangel. Gabriel I "believe" is an archangel, Michael, I "know" is an archangel! The word archangel really means chief or principal messenger. In Daniel's writing, Michael is seen as "The great prince, which standeth for the children of thy people" (Daniel 12:1; 10:21). "Michael, your prince." If you want to picture the prominence of the archangel, read again I Thessalonians 4:16. He is with the Lord Jesus!

Gabriel is mentioned more than Michael in Scripture, but never is called an archangel. He seems to be God's special newsbearer. The name Gabriel has three meanings in Hebrew. "God is great," "God is here" and "The Mighty One." Tradition, as is the case so many times, has handed down lies rather than truth. You might ask any American, "Who is going to blow the horn on judgement day?" and the answer would be Gabriel. Songwriters write of him blowing a horn. Any reference to this might be when Jesus returns for the Church and with the "trump of God." All else is speculation.

For Scripture's sake, put the horn out of your mind when you think of Gabriel. He is God's bearer of good news. He is mentioned only four times in God's Word and, each time, he brings news from heaven. Twice in the Old Testament he brought news to Daniel (Daniel 8:16; 9:21). His news concerned the end time and is worthy of study. Twice in the New Testament Gabriel appeared: to Zacharias to announce the birth of John the Baptist, (Luke 1: 13); and to Mary to announce the birth of the Lord Jesus (Luke 1:31). Gabriel may blow a horn, but God's Word does not say so. He is God's special messenger.

The cherubim are the first mentioned in God's Word (Genesis 3:24). They were placed at the East of the Garden of Eden with a flaming sword. Cherubim is plural for the word cherub. They are in my estimation the most mystical of the angelic creatures. Ezekiel gives detailed descriptions of the creatures in his vision; they are mentioned 21 times in chapter 10 alone. They are difficult to picture, because our finite minds have never seen anything similar. This much is clear about the cherubim. They have four wings, at least in some descriptions; four faces, full of eyes; they have feet and hands. They are carved symbolically upon the "Ark of the Covenant" in the Tabernacle and in the Temple of Solomon. They are powerful and in at least one passage they assume roles of "guardian angels" (Gen. 3:24). What if sinful man had found his way back into the Garden of Eden after sinning? Had he eaten of the Tree of Life in his sinful nature, he would live forever in a sinful body. The cherubim have successfully guarded the garden.

One other truth about this being is that its heavenly position is "beside the throne" (see Psalm 80:1 and Psalm 99:1).

"Thou dwellest between the cherubim" and "He sitteth between the cherubim." The seraphim are found by name only in Isaiah, chapter six. I recently preached from this chapter. It is a picture of someone coming from heaven with the ability to cleanse from sin. Jesus is seen on every page! What Isaiah saw in his vision was "the Lord sitting upon a throne, high and lifted up." If you ever "see" the Lord it will be just as it is written here, reigning as Lord of all, "high and lifted up." Isaiah saw, standing above the throne, "the seraphim." He did not mention the cherubim in his vision, but we have learned among other things, that the cherubim stand beside the throne. God's throne is surrounded by angelic creation. Note an interesting statement in Isaiah 6:3, "…the whole earth is full of his glory." The glory of God is not limited to the throne, the heavenlies, but the "whole earth is full of His glory." Why don't we see it?

The seraphim are described briefly: each one had six "wings"; "His face," "His Feet" are mentioned. The seraphim also used two of their wings to fly. How long does it take an angel to descend from God's throne to man's presence? Possibly faster than the speed of light! In a flash, Isaiah records the seraphim leaving God's throne to touch the lips of this self-proclaimed "unclean man." Notice the angel did not touch the "live coal from off the altar," but the "live coal" touched Isaiah. It changed Isaiah. He was cleansed and surrendered after a touch from the altar of God.

Again, we can see the angels move at God's direction. The seraphim appear to have at least three functions.

(1) Praising God; each one said to the other "Holy, Holy, is the Lord of Hosts."

(2) They stand above the throne, perhaps in a guardian role much as the cherubim.

(3) They minister to man as God sees fit.

There is no indication as to how many seraphim were created or if they are perhaps mentioned somewhere in other Scripture as simply "angels." The meaning of the word seems to be interpreted "love," though scholars are not certain. It is clear that the three functions mentioned, of the seraphim are also the duties of other angels. I suppose they can be distinguished best by their position "above the throne," and their chief duty is to praise God. I believe that, too, is the chief duty of man. I don't believe we praise Him enough! The whole earth is full of his glory.

Guardian angels are possibly the area of greatest interest to man. Each of us has heard the phrase "guardian angel" in a personal sense, "my" or "your" guardian angel. To my knowledge the two words are not found together in Scripture. Most of doctrine taught by man concerning these angelic beings comes from childhood stories, songwriters, poets and painters. Who has not seen a picture of a small child crossing a bridge under the watchful eye of an angel? A Catholic priest told me recently, "It is the position of the Catholic church that everyone has at least one protecting angel."

Our reason for believing in angels must be scripturally anchored. What does God's Word say? Matthew 18:10 "Take heed that ye despise not one of these little ones; for I [Jesus] say unto you, that in heaven *their angels* do always behold the face of my Father which is in heaven." Now I know the seraphim and the cherubim are positioned so as to see the Father's face. They qualify as "guardian angels." This I know. Jesus said that from my birth I had an angel beholding the face of God the Father, ready to move at His command. Man is warned in this chapter (Matt. 18), not to offend a little one. I believe further that the little one is protected from eternal damnation by God's wonderful grace.

Matthew 18:1-3 seems to make it clear not only that the little children in their innocence are secure in God's grace but also a picture of what Jesus does in the salvation of man: "...except ye converted and become as little children, ye shall not enter the Kingdom of Heaven." So the question seems to be now, what happens when a child reaches that mystical "age of accountability" and rejects Jesus? Does he lose that angelic protection? I must say, I do not know. The Bible does not say. However, if that is true the angel or angels return at salvation, for they are all "ministering spirits sent to minister for the heirs of salvation."

Earlier I related the details of my youngest child who asked God to let him see "his" angels. I told of the detailed description of what he saw and heard! May I simply say the seraphim and cherubim fit in the realm of "guardian angels" and I believe angels minister for me, by faith in God's unerring Word. Read Matthew 18:10 again and think upon it as you read the following article. This story was carried by the major news services and this particular article appeared in the Dallas Morning News.

"A five year old girl said she was awakened by an angel.

61

She was credited with saving her sleeping family from a fire which destroyed their mobile home Tuesday in Foil, Okla. Mr. & Mrs. George Wilcox said their daughter, Rosa, rushed into their room about 4 a.m. yelling there was a fire in the residence. Mrs. Wilcox said her daughter prays before going to sleep for "an angel to watch over her." When asked how she managed to wake up and warn her family, Rosa said the angel told her about the fire."

Admittedly, "guardian angel" may not be the appropriate term or theologically correct in the eyes of scholars. Personally, I like the term; it is well supported by Scripture as to the duty of angels. I am made happy to know that whatever you call them, God's Holy angels do minister to man. I like the phrase my young son used to tell me of angels. "I asked God to show me 'my' angels." Read Matthew 18:10 again, "in heaven *their* angels..." Believer, be encouraged, God's Holy angels are round about us. Believe it!

Jesus said, "Thinkest thou that I cannot pray to my Father, and he shall presently give me more than twelve legions of angels?" If each of those angels possessed the same power as the "one" angel who slew 185,000 men, the thought becomes awesome! Jesus could have beckoned for a heavenly army with capabilities of slaying at least 13,320,000,000 or 13 billion people! That's more than twice the world's present population.

Angels abound in multitude and might!

Chapter 6

METHODS AND MOTIVES

Numbers 20: 6 *And when we cried unto the Lord, he heard our voice, And sent an angel, and hath brought us forth out of Egypt...*

Dr. J. Vernon McGee, for years pastor of the Church of the Open Door in Los Angeles and radio speaker on over 500 stations, made the following statement: "When God chose to speak to man in the Old Testament times, he spoke thru the angel of the Lord." Now there is a question often asked, is the "angel of the Lord" in the Old Testament "really" the pre-incarnate Christ? Dr. McGee said, "This angel of the Lord was none other than the Lord Jesus speaking in the form of an angel." In Dr. McGee's respected opinion there is no doubt, the angel of the Lord is the second person of the Trinity, Jesus, in angelic form.

The Angel of the Lord! If we are to understand the Scripture concerning angels, I believe it is necessary to believe that the Old Testament references to "the angel" of the Lord, is indeed, God the Son manifest in angelic form. Now this, of course, would make "the angel" of the Lord, highest in rank if we class him with the angels. But He is not to be classed as a created angel, rather, the Creator of the angels. Old Testament study will reveal that God used angels or He appeared as angel to make His will known to men. It was His method of communicating His will to man. Hebrews 13:8 is sufficient for me not to be troubled in either case. Scripture declares, "Jesus Christ the same yesterday, and today, and forever." Bible scholars have written volumes about this, but most of the argument is no more than "splitting hairs" concerning the doctrine of "the angel of the Lord."

I could draw from these volumes and share it with you, but this is not in line with my purpose here. My intention is to cause believers to *believe more* and to *doubt less;* to create an awareness of God's presence; to simplify the subject of angels. Therefore, I will reserve my comments on "the angel of the Lord" lest it cause confusion.

Regardless, "the angel of the Lord" fits in the *Method and Motive* of angelic visits. He appears. He speaks. He departs. He reappears.

Old Testament accounts reveal that the angels were active in Abraham's life, from his calling out of Ur of the Chaldees (Genesis 15:7), to his death at age 175 (Gen. 25:7). Angelic messengers brought news to Abraham and Sarah that they should bear a son. In chapter 16, "the angel of the Lord" found Sarah by a fountain of water in the wilderness (Gen. 16:7-11). Four times, "the angel of the Lord" speaks here, much like Gabriel: he brought a name for Abraham's son by his handmaid Hagar. "Thou shalt call his name Ishmael...and he will be a wild man; his hand will be against every man, and every man's hand against him..." (16:11,12). From Ishmael came the Arabic Muslim nations.

Sodom and Gomorrah is another instance mentioned where the Angel of the Lord appeared unto him (Abraham). "In the heat of the day; and he lift up his eyes and looked, and lo, three men stood by him..." (Genesis 18:1,2). The angels here appeared as men, they ate with Abraham and Sarah and reassured them that they would bear a son. In Sarah's doubt, one of the angels spoke to her similarly as Gabriel did to Mary. "Is anything too hard for the Lord?" (Gen. 18:14). Gabriel told Mary, "With God all things are possible." One of these three angels "seems" to be God manifest or the Angel of the Lord. For Abraham prayed that Sodom and Gomorrah would be spared after hearing the angels pronounce judgement on the cities.

In Genesis 19:1, the Scripture clearly states that "two angels" came to Sodom. The entire account of Sodom and Gomorrah tells us that these two angels took up the forms of men, but had judgement powers. The angels warned of destruction to come. They could not act until God willed. Fire and brimstone from heaven destroyed the city as forewarned by the angels. They were accurate in their messages from heaven!

Isaac, Abraham's son, could tell of the heavenly visitors. It was in Abraham's faith trial that his young son, bound and upon the altar of sacrifice, heard an angelic voice (Gen. 22:11). The voice brought joy to both father and son for the angel announced redemption, a substitute; God provided a sacrifice! What news to the ears of Abraham and Isaac.

Moses, God's great deliverer! The "burning bush," and the multitudes of miracles performed through him by the Lord. Again volumes could be written, but let Moses speak,

"And when we cried unto the Lord, he heard our voice, and sent an angel, and hath brought us forth out of Egypt..." (Numbers 20:16).

Think back to that night of deliverance. Moses had delivered God's message, as he had received it, to Pharaoh. That midnight hour, God would send His angel, or angels, to claim the first-born from all of Egypt. God speaks and there is life. He also has the final word at death. At God's command the angel, or angels, swept over the land. They were looking for the blood! They still minister to those under the blood! If they did not find the bloodstained wood, their heavenly instructions were to take life from the first-born of every household. More will be said about angels and death in a subsequent chapter.

Balaam is another instance where the Angel of the Lord is mentioned. Ten times there is reference to the Angel of the Lord in Numbers, chapter 22. The Angel of the Lord moved here because "God's anger was kindled..." (Num. 22:22). This is an interesting intervention by heaven. The Lord allowed a donkey to see an angel. He allowed the donkey to speak to his master. The donkey saw an angel with his sword drawn! Even a donkey can recognize his own master. This is perhaps the most unusual of all heavenly angelic appearances. Read the account and count the many ways God did intervene. The angel of the Lord stood in the way; he turned Balaam, the donkey, and the two servants aside. Yes, God's angels intervene in the affairs of man. If God so chooses, he can allow animals a glimpse of the heavenlies. God is sovereign and I'm glad.

The account of the three Hebrew Children, is one of

the favorite stories of God's children down through the ages and gives some insight into "the Angel of the Lord" question. Shadrach, Meshack, and Abednego refused to serve another God. They were convinced that standing for right was right! They knew their God was able and trusted their lives completely in His hands (Daniel, chapter 3). They were bound and cast into a "burning fiery furnace." They were not scarred, marred, or charred, for God "sent his angel." The angel was seen by the Babylonians and was described in form as the Son of God. The angel was God-sent and he arrived right on time!

And what about Daniel? Now Daniel is possibly as well known as any Old Testament character. Even little children with just a little Sunday school exposure know of this man. I will ask a question: What comes to your mind immediately when you hear the name Daniel, the lion's den, right? But did you know about the angel in the lion's den? Daniel was framed by his jealous peers, and because he refused to cease from praying he was cast into the den of lions...hungry lions. Hungry lions eat people, but they did not touch Daniel. Why? Daniel said, "My God hath sent His Angel, and hath shut the lions' mouths..." (6:22). Lock that thought in your mind, "My God hath sent His Angel..." Daniel was given prophecy concerning Jesus, and the end time. In one vision, in chapter 8, Daniel could not discern the meaning of the vision. In verses 15 and 16, "...there stood before him as the appearance of a man and I [Daniel] heard a man's voice...which said, 'Gabriel, make this man to understand the vision.' " Gabriel was sent to reveal the meaning of the vision.

In Daniel, chapter 10:3, Daniel had prayed for three weeks,

mourning and fasting. His answer did not come, but it was on the way. God had sent an angel to answer Daniel's prayer but the fallen angels delayed the answer. There was fighting in the heavenlies. Look at verses 12, 13, the angel says, "from the first day you prayed God heard and I am come for thy words. But the prince of the kingdom of Persia withstood me 'twenty-one' days; but, Michael one of the chief princes, came to help me..." (see v. 21). The angel departs, declaring, "I will return to fight..." The little phrase "one of the chief princes" is to further indicate that there are many, mighty, powerful angels. Perhaps they even possess similar powers as Michael. However, Michael, is the only angel referred to as *the* archangel.

If we could see the invisible war going on about us, we would surely be frightened above our strength to withstand. The war rages with Lucifer and his fallen angels interfering at every opportunity with God's Holy angels intervening and ministering. I'm glad I know where the victory lies and happy to be "among" the Lord's Redeemed.

In chapter 12, "end time" prophecy is spoken (v.1), and at that time shall Michael stand up..."; (v. 9) "Go thy way Daniel; for the words are closed up and sealed till the time of the end." Victory! Angels brought news of ultimate victory. When Michael stands with heaven's host, Armaggedon will climax. Lucifer and his fallen angels will meet their ultimate doom finalized in the "Lake of Fire."

What can we learn from these Old Testament accounts as to the method and motive of angels? Their method is almost always the same. They appear, deliver their message, and depart. Whatever their form of appearance, they are always recognized as "from God." Isaiah and Ezekiel saw creatures with wings; Abraham and Jacob describe them as men; but they were always recognized as being sent from God. Their function is always to minister and/or to bring a message from heaven. Their motive is to please God in obedience.

David, in the Psalms speaks much about the angels, and David is credited with writing most of the Psalms. In Psalm 8:5 we a reminded that we are created "a little lower than angels." It is in the Psalms that we learn that angels possibly eat; food that man also can eat. It is not angels food cake, but manna (Ps. 78:25), "Man did eat angels' food; God sent them meat to the full."

A Psalm not attributed to David, but speaking a great truth of God's angels is Psalm 80:1 "...thou that dwell between the cherubim, shine forth." Psalm 91:11 is Scripture that Lucifer himself referred to in his temptation of Jesus. "For he shall give his angels charge over thee keep thee in all thy ways."

The Old Testament refers to angels at least 105 times and their methods and motives are consistent. Even the closing book of the Old Testament has angels implied in its name, for Malachi means "My messenger," and messenger is another word for angel.

For just a glimpse of angelic power you might read II Kings 19:35, one angel killed 185,000 men of Assyrian army. Jesus had over 70,000 ready to come in the garden prior to His crucifixion.

Those who ignore Old Testament truths find no value in studying the account of old. To those of you who are so inclined please note the consistency of angels' methods and motives in the Old and New Testament.

I purposely did not mention Jacob, but will in a future chapter. Obviously, I could not deal with every angelic experience. What does the New Testament reveal? Angels are mentioned at least 165 times in 39 books, and by my count are mentioned 66 times in the book of Revelation alone.

The angels were active prior to the birth of Christ. Gabriel was sent from God and both Mary and Zacharias saw him. Now, Gabriel is not described, but was recognized as from God and he brought a message from heaven! Read just 20 verses into the New Testament and an angel appears to Joseph "in a dream." He brought a message and was recognized as being sent from God. I believe there will be much angelic activity that precedes the second coming and there will also be an increase of demonic activity as the world is being prepared for the anti-christ. We live in the most exciting days of all of Church history!

If God were going to speak to you or me through an angel, would he send an "agent" that we would not recognize from God? No! God would not confuse a believer; Satan is the author of confusion. There was never a doubt in the lives of those who saw angels; they brought sweet assurance with their presence. I believe if an angel were to appear to me, it would be in the form of what I picture angels to be; they are spirits and when visible they take on a recognizable form. They are superior in intellect and I am convinced that the angels' methods and motives have not changed. They still appear, speak, and disappear! But never aside from or in conflict with God's completed revelation, the Bible!

The angels ministered to Jesus. Multitudes gathered at His birth. Praising God and making heavenly announcements. They directed Mary and Joseph to Egypt and back to Galilee. Looking after the little Lord Jesus! Matthew in his gospel moves swiftly from the young Jesus to His Baptism and the beginning of His ministry.

They did not help during His temptation, although Satan urged Jesus to call upon them. They stood ready (Matt. 4), but Jesus had to endure that alone. However, they were quick to come immediately after the Devil left "...angels came and ministered unto him."

In Matthew 13:41, Jesus refers to the angels as "his angels." In Matthew 18:10 Jesus refers to little children as having "their angels." Jesus spoke much of the angels and He gives us additional information about them:

> (1) They do not marry (Matt. 22:30).
> (2) They are not omniscient.
> (3) They don't know when the end shall be.
> (4) They share in God's knowledge on a limited basis (Matt.24:36).
> (5) They are the heavenly escorts of the saints at death (Matt. 24:31).

The account of the rich man and Lazarus is a beautiful picture of this in Luke 16:22,23. And Jesus, when He went to the Garden of Gethsemane, He took His closest disciples and they could not help, instead, they slept. But as He prayed, "...nevertheless not my will, but thine, be done, and there appeared an angel unto him from heaven, strengthening him" (Luke 22:42, 43).

The angels stood ready to come to His rescue as soldiers approached with swords and staves. As Peter was quick to fight for His Lord, Jesus mentioned that 72,000 angels stood waiting for His beckoning call. The angels could not come! He must die alone! And He did! Because He did, there is a song I can sing that even angels cannot. They are not redeemed. Jesus is their Creator, Lord and Master. He is my Creator, Savior, Lord and Master. The angels were quick to come after the 72 hours in the grave.

One angel rolled away the stone. Angels announced His resurrection and, according to Matthew 28:2-7, they were anxious for the news to be spread. "He is not here; for He is risen ...go quickly and tell ...lo, I have told you."

As Jesus left the earth, ascending to heaven, the angels came to announce His coming back, for Acts 1:11, declares "...this same Jesus, which is taken up from you into heaven, shall so come in like manner as ye have seen him go into heaven." Amen.

Angels and their ministry, their methods and motives have just begun! Jesus has made it possible for man to be "heirs of salvation" and the Scripture declares that the angels are "...all ministering spirits *sent forth* to minister for them who shall be heirs of salvation" (Heb. 1:14).

Peter was an heir of salvation and angels were active in his life. He was put in prison for preaching the Gospel, "But the angel of the Lord opened the prison doors, and brought them forth and said, Go, stand and speak in the temple to the people all the words of this life."

Phillip was sent an angel from the Lord in Acts 8:26, and the angel told him to leave Samaria and go unto Gaza, which is desert. Phillip did not question. He obviously recognized the angel as a heavenly messenger!

Cornelius was a Gentile and angels now are speaking to an Italian named Cornelius, Acts 10:1-7. The angel appeared, gave his message (he had come because Cornelius' prayer had reached God), and departed. The methods and motives of the angels are still unchanged.

Paul, the great apostle, spoke of angels often. He spoke of an angelic language in I Corinthians 13:1. He mentions Satan being an angel of light and having his own ministers (II Cor. 11:14, 15). He mentions that even an angel from heaven cannot preach any other gospel without being accursed (Gal. 1:8).

In the midst of a terrible storm and shipwreck Paul proclaimed that the "angel of God" had stood by him that night and assured him none of the 276 souls abroad would be lost. The angel was right on time! They cannot fail! They are God's Holy angels!

John, while on the Isle of Patmos, speaks of angels often in the Book of Revelation. I will say little about John's experience. Not because it is unimportant, but space does not allow. John saw angels; he heard angels; he questioned angels; he recorded their message; he saw angels in roles of judgement, wrath and doom; he saw the "grim reaper"; he saw Satan bound by one mighty angel.

The great truth I want to draw from his experience is that he was told not to worship them. Angels do not desire our worship. The angel said "Worship God" (Rev. 22:9). Their methods and motives continue today, ministering to men as directed by God. Angels stand all about us, ministering, working in and about our lives, not as the Holy Spirit, but in conjunction with Him, Holy angels under Holy direction. Whatever you are doing now, wherever you may be, angels look on, and though we may be totally "unaware," we entertain angels (Heb. 13:2).

Christian, stand tall in this confidence, their methods and motives have not changed!

Chapter 7

MYSTICAL MOMENTS

Genesis 32: 1 *"And Jacob went on his way, and
the angels of God met him."*

Who has not had an unexplainable occurrence in his life?
Almost everyone can recall an event that leads the person
to say, "I don't know why I wasn't killed!" "I should have
been seriously injured." Talk with almost anyone about
mystical events and they will have something to share. The
subject is popular!

Phenomena beyond our understanding stir interest in the
hearts of almost everyone. Something inside us wants to
grasp the supernatural. The world has gone into a complete
frenzy over movies and books on exorcism, Satanism, the
evil spirit world, etc. E.S.P. is always an interesting topic,
and even more so, the "Psychic Hotline." I asked an
acquaintance not long ago if he believed angels were still
active today. He was really not even interested, but said,
"No, I don't think so." Someone asked him if he believed
in E.S.P. "Yes," he said. "I don't understand it, but I have
experienced it."

Experiencing certainly lends to believing. During their childhood years, one of my sons was injured while playing. His head was gashed open blood covered his little face and my clothes, as I gathered him into my arms and as my wife drove us to the emergency room. He was frantic and in some pain. My wife and other son were concerned and upset; I was concerned as I watched the doctor put stitches into my son's bleeding head. That evening, after a very trying day and upsetting experience, before we went to bed, the phone rang. It was 10:30 p.m. The call came from Georgia; it was 11:30 there. It was my wife's mother. She said, "Is everything all right? I just could not sleep. I had the strangest feeling something was wrong." Did God send an angel "unaware?" I do not understand these happenings, but they are numerous!

Duke University has volumes written on research into these types of "phenomena." They have documentation on a host of similar experiences with no valid explan-ations. I recall while in high school an experience that was very real to my baseball teammates and me. Our high school team had traveled from Haltom High School across town to North Side High School in Fort Worth. Their baseball field was built in such a manner that the cyclone fence backstop and dugout were very close to home plate and to the "on deck" position for the next batter.

The game began and I was the second batter. Our team occupied the third base dugout and our lead off batter was right-handed. I took my position in the on-deck circle. There was very little space between the fence where I knelt and the batters' box. However, a right-handed batter seldom fouls a ball directly behind him. There was no thought of danger in my mind. Only as I look back does it cause me to be mindful of God's Presence.

Our batter swung at the first pitch; he hit the ball and splintered his bat. As his swing was completed, the jagged end of the splintered bat came loose and flew directly at my head. "Somehow" I managed to move and the bat rammed as a spear into the aluminum fence directly behind me. I know "something" moved me. My teammates and coach remarked of how it appeared I was jerked to the ground. It happened and I can't explain how I fell to the ground so quickly. You say, reflex action. I don't know. But as I think back on that, from time to time, I see angels intervening as the Devil tried to kill me.

I am convinced you could tell me a similar story in your life. But can you explain it? Angels watch when we don't, and when we can't. The disciples could not hold open their "weary, heavy eyes" at the garden, but the angels watched and ministered when the disciples couldn't. (Luke 22:43)

A pastor friend told me of an experience he had while a young child about 12 years old. He had an aunt who had raised him from a child and told how each morning she would come to his bed, touch him, and say, "Get up." He told that he had been trained to arise each morning from that touch and that voice, saying simply, "Get up." His aunt died and, in the pastor's words, "I know she was dead because I was at the cemetery when she was buried." He described the humble dwelling where this black Mississippi family was raised. "A huge Chinaberry tree grew just outside my bedroom window, and the roots came directly under my bed." While sound asleep late one spring evening, a storm came, tornado winds came through the area where they lived. "In the midst of the storm, while I was asleep, 'someone' touched me and said, 'Get up.' I opened my eyes and got out of bed, it was my 'aunt.' I followed her into the hall and she disappeared." He then said, "As soon as she was gone, that storm hit the huge Chinaberry tree and ripped it from the ground, the roots drove the bed where I was sleeping right through the roof." "Did God send an angel?" I asked. "Yes, oh yes, there was no other voice or touch that I would have obeyed other than my aunt's. I had been trained that way. I definitely believe God sent an angel in a form I would recognize and obey." Angels are superior in intellect and strength; I believe they move and operate in such mystical ways that we will not understand, until "they" escort us into God's presence.

Jacob is a difficult character to understand in Scripture. He connived and cheated his own brother. He deceived his aged father with the help of his mother. However, he was in the line of Abraham and in the Holy linage of Jesus. He ran from his brother's pursuit, he avoided opportunities to get right with God. If you are a part of God's plan and program, He is able to persuade you. There is a beautiful picture here in Jacob's life and experience.

In Jacob's deceit, God's angels dealt with him until he repented and walked with God. If Satan could have killed Jacob, he could have dented God's plan for redemption. Satan was on a leash then and is now. Through Esau, Satan sought to find and kill Jacob.

While running from Esau, Jacob found he was not moving away from God. In chapter 28 of Genesis, Jacob dreamed

(v. 12), *"And behold a ladder set up on the earth, and the top of it reached to heaven; and behold the angels of God ascending and descending on it."* At the top of the ladder, Jacob saw the Lord and was reassured of God's promises. The angels again bringing messages of assurance, caused Jacob to say in verse 17, *"...this is none other but the house of God, and this is the gate of Heaven."* Jacob's life was about to be changed by God through the ministry of angels. In Genesis 31:11-13, *"the angel of God spake unto him in a dream, saying...return unto the land of thy kindred."*

As Jacob journeyed (Gen. 32:1,2), *"...the angels of God met him. And when Jacob saw them, he said, 'This is God's host...' "* Jacob prayed and came unto the Lord in humility (v.10); he asked for deliverance, (v.11); and he claimed God's promises (v.10-12). God brought Jacob to the place we all must come to, if we are to please the Lord. Alone with God! Read Genesis 32:24-32. "And Jacob was left alone." Getting alone with God is necessary for God to speak to our lives! While alone with God, *"...there wrestled a man with him until the breaking of the day."* Was this an angel, was it "the angel of the Lord"? The angels had been active in Jacob's life; now he came in contact with such a heavenly being he did not want to turn loose. He wanted to be blessed. Blessings are God-given. I personally believe this is the pre-incarnate Christ, the angel of the Lord.

Jacob's name was changed to Israel, his walk was changed, and he proclaimed, in verse 30, *"...I have seen God face to face, and my life is preserved."* Jacob's angelic experiences brought him closer to God. Angels intervening in man's life today will bring him closer to God. Angels are all ministering spirits whose purpose still is to glorify God.

Why did I mention Jacob here? Two reasons:

(1) He is a picture of God working in a ruined, sinful life and making it righteous in God's sight.
(2) If Jacob related these experiences to you or to a modern-day psychologist, what would be the reaction?

A ladder going into heaven and angels going up and down the ladder? I think the boy needs psychiatric help. He's not getting enough rest. He has become psychotic. Jacob needs medical attention.

An angel telling you in a dream to leave this land and go to another? Sure, Jacob, sure!

Angels meeting him on the way, and him recognizing them as "God's Host." Wrestling with an angel all night. Jacob's name and life were changed! Visions? Heavenly voices speaking? One thing is undeniable; Jacob's name and Jacob's life were changed! All who knew could not deny that something happened. Jacob called it "God's Host," heavenly messengers, acting as directed from heaven.

Not long ago, I was asked to give my opinion to a member of my Sunday school class. He had some questions about a mysterious occurrence in his family's life. He told me that a few years ago his father was involved in a very serious accident while driving a truck. "It happened in another section of the country," he said, "but it happened at 3:30

a.m." and that was the mystery.

He told me that at precisely the time his father was in the terrible wreck, his mother was awakened and sensed that something was wrong. Also in another part of the country, his aunt was also awakened at the same time with the same feeling of "something's wrong."

Did God send an angel to awaken and create the awareness of "something's wrong?" I don't know. I could never be certain. I do know it is possible, probable, and in line with the angelic ministry.

Let me say again at this point, I have never seen an angel. I have had experiences that cause my faith in God's angelic ministers to increase.

I have never put much thought into dreams or into those who analyze dreams. However, I have had an undeniable experience witnessed by a host of friends and the congregation of the Wesley Evangelical Methodist Church in Hurst, Texas.

I have preached at this church on various occasions, so a portion of what I am to relate to you may not seem mysterious. I was scheduled to preach one Sunday when the Pastor was on vacation. The Saturday night before I had the most realistic dream of my life! In my dream, segments of the morning worship service to come were revealed to me. I experienced this first hand.

I have a dream. No, I guess it's better to say that I had a dream. In the dream, just before I preached, a friend of mine sang a song I had written. The song was "What a Day It Must Have Been, The Day My Savior Died." Also, in the dream the message I preached was this same title and same thought; it was very clear. In the dream, at invitation time, the music director led the congregation in the great hymn, "Only Trust Him." Now in this church, an altar rail separates the preacher from the congregation. However, in my dream, I walked around this rail to the front of the pulpit and during the invitation hymn, a young man came forward and someone with him; here the dream began to fade and my only recollection was that the young man told me (in the dream) he was in the Armed Services.

The dream was so real that when I awoke that morning, I took my Bible and turned to Matthew, chapter 27, a message was burning in my heart. I knew what I must preach. I called my friend and asked him to sing. I related part of my dream. He agreed to sing. When I arrived at the church, I requested that the music director sing "Only Trust Him " for the altar call.

As the services began I looked over the congregation to see if there was anyone there in uniform: Army, Navy, Marine, Air Force. I didn't see anyone. As my friend came to sing he related a portion of the dream to the congregation and his reason for being there.

I preached, I felt God's presence, but no more than at other times. As the invitation hymn was sung I made my way around the altar to the front of the pulpit and to the center aisle. Soon a young woman came forward and trusted Jesus as her Savior. The thoughts of the dream had left my mind completely. Then a young man came; he was her fiance and he came to rededicate his life. The invitation closed and I remained there with the couple as members came by to shake their hands and welcome them into God's family. It was then that the first woman, who came by, with tears in her eyes, pulled my head close to where she could speak through her tears. As she whispered she told me, "If I don't whisper. I'll shout. That young man is the only person in this congregation in the Armed Services and we have been praying for him and his girl friend for months!"

Then, I wanted to shout. My friend had already left the church but I called him as soon as I arrived home and said, "Guess, what happened?" He said, "I know, the man who came was in the Armed Services just as you dreamed." He said, "When you spoke to me of the dream I knew it was of God. I don't know how I knew, I just did."

Did God send an angel; was the Holy Spirit the only Holy function involved? I don't know. I do know God spoke to me through a dream. The revelation was not apart from His Word, but all in line with it. Now lest you get the wrong idea, let me say this is not something I boast in, nor do I go to sleep each night expecting another God-sent dream. I do want to make a distinction. I have dreamed, I suppose, as most people do, just dreams. I have also had some totally silly dreams. I want you to understand this; if God speaks to you through a dream, you will know it! Just as the angels of God, scripturally are always recognized by believers as heaven-sent. God will not confuse. He will not speak apart from His completed revelation, His Word. Our only checkpoint need be His Word. The "mystical moments" of life cannot be understood by man's most sophisticated computers, or by man's most respected intellects.

The weight of evidence of the spirit world cannot be discounted and in most cases cannot be understood. Satan is at work; his demons, though inferior to God's Holy angels, are at work and their work is to confuse, to take man's eyes off Jesus. They have power to reveal future events to man and they have power (though all is limited) over elements.

Beware of the mysterious, mystical moments, if they cause you to turn from Jesus. Fortune-telling is not of God! Ouija boards, as innocent as they may seem, can open doorways to demons. Witchcraft, good luck charms, superstition, etc., all have their roots in Hell and they are not of God!

Be sure, if God speaks, you will know it is of God. Christianity is not dependent upon mystical experiences. Faith and God's grace are the necessary ingredients. If God so chooses to work through your life by supernatural experiences, praise Him! Angels are often involved in mystical moments.

Chapter 8

MY MESSAGE

II Cor. 4:6 *For God, who commanded the light to shine out of darkness, hath shined in our hearts, to give the light of the knowledge of the glory of God in the face of Jesus Christ.*

I did not write this book to glorify the angels! Nor did I write it to bring attention to my family or myself. God forbid! My message is to glorify God, surely. . ."He has shined in my heart". Let me recall my son's experience again and give it scriptural checkpoints. He and I were both the subject of many prayers by many of God's people.

1. He had read Matthew 18:10. It told him "he" had angels before God and he believed it.
2. He asked God, expecting to see them.
3. He was not afraid.
4. He knew they were from God.
5. He has never read about any cherubim or seraphim (4-winged and 6-winged beings), but I had. This assured me.
6. He talked with them.
7. They gave their names.
8. They were masculine in form.

9. They were pleased to hear the name of Jesus.

10. Each appearance was to calm and assure; there was no message given outside of Scripture.

11. He had no desire to talk of them, but of Jesus.

12. He had not changed physically, withdrawn, nor become boastful, etc.

13. He was never confused. (God is not the author of confusion.)

14. He became more loving.

I5. He talked more of things that glorify Jesus.

16. He would not encourage others to desire to see angels. (He did not ask his mother, brother, or myself to ask God to let us see angels.)

17. He does not "desire" to see them now.

18. He is satisfied God did as God chose to do.

19. He said he thanked God and told Him he did not need to see them anymore.

20. He developed a great understanding about angels.

Further, he responded to adult questions (not necessarily directed to him) with statements such as: "You don't pray to angels. Angels don't want you to worship them." He gave his opinion as to why Lucifer fell from heaven. "Lucifer thought he was so beautiful and powerful that he thought the other angels would follow him instead of God." He has numerous insights about the angels, mainly, "They want you to worship God."

He became tenderhearted and caring. Today he is a neurosurgeon. In summary, I could say simply, the experience did not confuse him, but strengthened him in his faith. All that happened was positive! What did it mean to me?

God shined in my heart and I began to see God's Holy angels working all about me. Not with my eyes, but with my faith. I visited a friend named Marv Carter in the hospital soon after this "bathing in God's grace." He had a cyst removed from his spine. His doctor told him he would be in the hospital at least ten days and off work at least three months. The day after surgery his doctor told him the operation went much better than he expected and he would be home in a few days and off work maybe six weeks. I could visualize angels directing the surgeon's hands, moving the scalpel in a supernatural way. Marv will testify to God's goodness, the Holy Spirit's comfort, the answering of prayer and, "the angels coming to minister to him."

A few days after the angels appeared to my son he was injured while playing outside. His little face was all bloody, his hands clutching at his head in pain. Blood dripped from his wounded head; it covered me as I held him close to me. We arrived at the emergency room and he was near panic, screaming, "Don't let go! Dad, don't let go!" He screamed with every stitch the doctor took in his head. At one point he said, "Dad, where are they?" I didn't know how to explain to him. I just said, "They are here." The doctor completed the sutures and while cleaning his head, Robby's tears ceased; he turned loose of my arms that he had gripped so tightly. He sat up and started to get off of the emergency room table, but the doctor would not let him. "Where were they?" he wondered. "They" were guiding every move the doctor made.

I believe this with all of my heart. Robby told me, "As soon as the nurse, (it was a woman doctor), finished, I saw them standing in the corner of the room, looking at me and smiling." His fear was turned to a "calm assurance" that everything was ok! Where were the angels when he was injured? Why did they allow it? I really don't know at this point. I wish I did. I do know that Satan would kill my children, my wife, you, and myself if he had his way. He is inferior! He fails! God is superior! He cannot fail! His Holy angels cannot fail! I will not question.

Perhaps there was a tender loving lesson for us to learn. At any rate, I grew from the experience; so did Robby. He felt some of the pain that Jesus endured at Calvary. I saw some of the agony God the Father felt when Jesus cried, "My God, My God, why hast thou forsaken me?" "Dad, don't let go!"

The angels did not fail; they always arrive right on time. My message is to all believers. Believe in God's ability to care for you. Believe it more than ever. Why, because we are heirs of salvation. His Holy Creation moves as He directs. He is Omniscient. He knows all of our needs. He is Omnipresent. He is always present. Think of that, always present. He is Immutable, the same yesterday, today, and forever, the God of Abraham, Isaac, Jacob, David, Peter, John, and Paul.

The Truth is, my God and has not changed! He is Omnipotent! That is, He is all-powerful. No man has yet proclaimed as Jesus did, "All power is given unto me in heaven and in earth" (Matt. 28: 18). No man could ever give honest thought to making such a statement. The proclamation belongs to Deity. "All Power," not just great power, but *all* power is His. Not just in certain areas, but in "heaven and earth."

Though this concerns the power of God, it would be wise to recall that it is God's moral and personal attributes that make Him what He is versus what He chooses to be. His Forgiving, Loving, Sweet Gracious Spirit is all too important to go unmentioned here.

The four power attributes of God are:
1. He is Omniscient (all knowing).
2. He is Omnipresent (everywhere present at all times).
3. He is Immutable (he never changes).
4. He is Omnipotent (all powerful).

Now, every Bible student knows this, but how does this relate to angels? The angels are His! They do not possess these attributes, but they are governed by them. Do you realize what this means? The angels, being ministering spirits are sent forth by God. The Holy angels cannot be misdirected because of their Director. They cannot act contrary to God's all-knowing will because it is through His knowledge of situations that they are sent.

The Holy angels are all about us because they are constantly praising God and His Spirit is everywhere present, at all times. The angels of God will act in my life and yours as quickly as they did in Abraham's, Jacob's, Daniel's, Peter's, Paul's, or John's, because this administrator is Immutable. He never changes! Just think of God never forgetting. He is so good! He is not a respecter of persons, a concept clearly taught in the Scriptures, but He can do as He chooses. He is bound only by His Word and that because He chooses to be.

My message to you concerning angels is to be aware of their presence and their ministering. Don't take a negative attitude toward the angelic ministry. If you have not seen or heard an angel, don't let that be reason to doubt. Don't be critical of Christians who have had experiences you don't understand or haven't had. Live and walk "by faith" and accept what the Lord wills for your life.

Not all are called of God to preach, teach, or sing, because God in His wisdom selects those that have special talents to do a special job. "We are members in particular" of His body. If God wants to deal with someone in a way you don't understand, you just live your life for Jesus and let the Holy Spirit and God's Word be your guide and gauge.

Why don't we see more of the supernatural? I have my personal opinions as to why many people are not aware of the angelic ministry. The church has become lax in its teaching and preaching of God's Holy angels! Believers have become less dependent upon God. They do not see Him. He is not "as real" as He would like to be in most lives.

There are no fires of persecution, no lion's dens, no fiery furnaces, no threats of prison and punishment to believers. We are no longer fed to the lions. Prayer meetings are less than genuine. Bible study is, many times, just so many words. We are content in our air- conditioned buildings. Selfish pastors and greedy congregations build "monuments to men." We worship in ignorance of God's glory and power. Seminaries have dulled the faith of many young preachers. Rationalism and psychological explanations are focused upon less than the supernatural.

Men who have suddenly discovered a "better translation" are tampering with the Bible. The vision of the average church and church member is a selfish vision.

It's little wonder that we cannot see God's Holy angels at work! My reasons are many but they all fit in this realm of selfishness. Surely God is not pleased that we choose to be so blind! I am going to tell the story of Jesus and I won't forget His Holy angels. They are working now. Would you read carefully the following Scripture? *"For I think God hath set forth us the apostles last, as it were appointed to death; for we are made a spectacle unto the world, and to angels, and to men"* (1 Cor. 4:9). We are made a spectacle; we are watched by the angels. The angels of God watch as we move and go on our way. There is no indication that the angels sleep. As we sleep, they watch. They are ready to move as God directs. Prayer causes the angels to act. Read Daniel, chapter 10. Daniel prayed; God sent an angel! I can testify to this not only by faith but also by experience.

I recall preaching at the Texas Department of Criminal Justice, Ferguson Unit. This particular unit is for first offenders and most of the some 2,000 inmates are between the ages of 18 and 21. Prison is a very solemn place to visit. There are not many smiles there; there is little to smile about. I personally visited with an inmate prior to preaching. I had been communicating with this newborn prisoner for sometime. In the course of our communicating, I sent him a brief summary of my son's "angelic experience." He told me as we talked that the news was all over the prison. I smiled, expressing some of the joy that it brought to my heart. I said, "Angels have been visiting prisons for a long time."

We talked about Daniel and the New Testament accounts of Peter, John, and Paul. His eyes beamed with excitement as we explored God's Word and he was assured that God's angels were present in his prison, in his cell. That is something to smile about. A few months later, I was visiting with a believer confined at the Federal Correctional Institute at Seagoville, Texas. We talked about many things from God's Word. As we talked, the inmate mentioned something about angels. Time did not permit me to share the experience and I simply mentioned that I had a personal testimony I would send him, the same brief summary I had sent to the other inmate. A few days later I received a letter from my friend at Seagoville. He said in his correspondence, "Brother Don...the news is all over the compound. I read the paper you sent in our chapel service. Before the evening was over I had the glorious privilege of leading seven (7) convicts to Our Lord. Praise God!"

Angels active in our prison system! Oh, that prisoners everywhere could learn of God's great love, of how his love extends beyond the prison walls. That His Holy angels stand ready to minister; to minister to believers everywhere, even in lonely prison cells. Guns and guards and cells with bars can't keep his Spirit out! Angels stand to meet your needs. God bless you, the inmates. Lonely believer, wherever and however you may be imprisoned, God loves you! I'm convinced that it would please our Lord if somehow we could share the positive message of God's glorious creation. If we would tell with beaming confidence, that Jesus loves and His love just keeps on reaching.

Once an inmate, in an effort to help me understand how terrible prison life was, began to tell of the guards' cruelty, their "low mentality," and to generally degrade all the guards. I listened and thought before I replied. I recalled seeing the guards stationed all about the units, doing their job, a very unpleasant job. After hesitating, I said, "God loves the officers the same and they have a very difficult job. He loves us all." The inmate smiled and said, "Yeah, man, I guess I just can't understand how much He does love."

Remember the jailer at Philippi? Jesus saved him and his family. (Acts 16).

Many years ago I went to John Peter Smith Hospital, a local county hospital, to visit a fellow worker. I had heard on the news that he had been shot. First reports indicated that he was shot while breaking and entering a home. Later reports said that he was a victim of robbery. All I really knew was that this man was a black friend of mine and the thing we had in common was belonging to Jesus.

He was married and his two young children were stricken with sickle cell anemia. He worked two jobs to help meet medical expenses, but he always had a smile and something kind to say. It is always depressing to go to a hospital, but more so the county hospital. People were standing in the halls waiting to be treated. I made my way through the crowd and to the staircase. I knew if my friend was guilty that he would be under police guard and I probably would have difficulty in seeing him. I came out of the third floor staircase and motioned to a couple of nurses who were glancing in my direction. Joel was in the ICU ward; I asked if they would take me to see him, explaining that I was a preacher

They led me down the long solemn hallway to a security area and the ICU ward, then through the doors to where my friend was. Somehow it didn't seem to matter to me if he was guilty; I felt certain that he wasn't, but I could even understand the possibility of life's pressures getting to him. I just wanted to tell him that I loved him, and Jesus loved him.

He had already undergone two operations. One bullet was removed from the back of his head and one from his shoulder. He smiled when he heard my voice and softly explained that he could not see very well. He was anxious to tell me what happened; unknown to me, the man who shot him had already been arrested. He said a "friend" went with him to the bank on his lunch hour. He needed $600-$700 to pay bills. He said, "My friend was going to leave town and had already checked in some luggage at the bus station and he said he would go with me to the bank before leaving. I guess he saw all the money and it just got to him. I just don't know." They drove to the man's house and Joel asked to use the telephone. "While I was dialing the number, he shot me in the back of the head and shoulder."

"As I was falling to the floor," he said, "My wife and children came to my mind, it seemed like a million times, it seemed like I was falling in slow motion, everything seemed to be slowed down. When I hit the floor, I pretended to be dead. I knew he would shoot me again if he thought I was alive. He dragged me to a closet first, but then decided not to leave me there. He dragged me outside

94

and toward the garage. I guess he was going to put me in the trunk and dump me somewhere, I don't know. I kept repeating the 23rd Psalm, over and over in my mind."

He said, "I gathered all the strength I could and began to kick and fight against him. It must have surprised him and he tried to get his gun. I ran across the street. No one was home, but praise God the door was open; I got inside before he could shoot me again. Somehow I managed to find the phone and called the police. I don't remember much after that ...except they told me I had a hole about the size of a silver dollar in the back of my head and would have to have a steel plate in about six months. I don't know what I'll do about my family. They need me. I thought I was about to get a promotion but I guess that's gone now." Still he smiled and said, "God will help me, won't He, Don?" "Yes," I replied. "His angels already have delivered you from the jaws of death and He will take care of you."

We had prayer together. He was patched up all over his upper body and his teeth had been damaged; he tried to eat but the food was dribbled all over his chest. He wanted to cry, but still he managed to smile. "Praise God!" He said, "God's angels gave me strength, Don. I know it was God's angels."

I left the ICU ward back through the mob of sick and concerned. Over and over in my mind I quoted the 23rd Psalm-one verse seemed to stand out, "Yea, though I walk through the valley of the shadow of death, I will fear no evil; for *thou art with me,* thy rod and thy staff they comfort me." I also thought of his last statement after we prayed. "God's Angels gave me strength, Don. I know it was God's

Angels."

I suppose the world is at this point almost deaf to the word "depression." Seems every one is taking something to remain somewhat stable and depression free. Isn't everyone depressed at one time or another? Is the word becoming commonplace? Perhaps the word is, but the fact of depression is so very real. It touches all of our lives. In my ministry I have been to many depressing places, been involved in many depressing situations. I have mentioned hospitals and prisons. Most of us are acquainted with hospitals, but unless you have spent some time with inmates, seen the cells and confining walls and the terrible loneliness, you can only imagine. The circumstances are such that you must "be there" to begin to understand.

Death and ugly surroundings are depressing. There are few words or expressions of comfort. Death is "just ugly" from the human standpoint. Nursing homes, orphan's homes, are not pretty sights and are a blemish on our society. Poverty, true poverty, is indescribably depressing. Though America is almost poverty-free by world standards, I have wept because of conditions in a home, maybe "house" is a better word. Once I stopped my car to give a "stale" sandwich to a hungry-looking dog. When I called the dog to the car, two small children came along with it, as it was their dog. I explained the sandwich was spoiled but they could feed it to their dog. As I drove away I looked in my rear view mirror, the little children were eating the sandwich as though they had not eaten in days. My heart broke, I wept and prayed, "God send your angels to the little ones."

Angels come at times of depression and they go to places of depression. They minister for our Lord. They minister for His children. Believing this can bring you out of a depressing situation with a smile of confidence. Of all the songs that I can recall singing about angels there is one that stands above the rest when I think of angels ministering for me. I don't suppose you would find it in the average church hymnal. I don't even know that song's title. The little phrase that I sing in my heart says, "All day, all night, angels watching over me, my Lord. All day, all night, angels watching over me."

How comforting to know that. All day and all night, that is all the time. Think about that and thank God that it is true. Angelic protection is an expression of God's great love for mankind. Yet it is just one of the many ways that God expresses His love. I can rejoice when I sing this song. It is a song of praise and thanksgiving. It makes me smile deep down inside when I sing "All day, all night, angels watching over me, my Lord. All day, all night, angels watching over me!"

Hitchcock's Topical Bible makes some general, but significant, statements. They serve as a quick reminder here of something already explored earlier. Angels: "are not to be worshiped, appear as men, are superhuman, wear human apparel, are untold in numbers, wait on God, they announce God's law, convey God's message, protect God's people, inflict God's penalties, are ministering spirits, are guardians of cities and nations, share in the counsel of God, sound the apocalyptic trumpets, and gather the elect to Judgement."

Among the Holy agents are "cherubim and seraphim" and "the angel of the Lord, or God as the pre-incarnate Christ." Now, I have already touched on all of these areas, some more than others. I have said little about the angels at death and clearly this is one of their chief roles. Luke 16:19-31 is most likely not just a parable; names of individuals are mentioned. Regardless, there is truth here about angels. "And it came to pass that the beggar died, and was carried by the angels into Abraham's bosom..." (v. 22). Lazarus was not only watched by God's Holy angels through his life, but they escorted him into eternal life.

In Matthew 13 there are several parables the disciples did not understand and questioned. In verse 39 Jesus said, "...the harvest is the end of the world; and the reapers are the angels." "The Son of Man shall send forth his angels, and they shall gather out of his kingdom all things that offend..." (v. 41). In verses 49,50, Jesus again spoke, "So shall it be at the end of the world; the angels shall come forth, and sever the wicked from the just, and shall cast them into the furnace of fire..."

Angels acting since their creation as God directs and since Cain killed Abel, angels have been active in "carrying the believer into God's presence."

I related earlier the death of a child stricken with leukemia. I told of his father being in the room when the child died, holding him in his arms, and feeling the final jerk of death. What I did not tell was what the pastor-father saw just prior to the child's death. The pastor had sat up with his dying child all night and had eventually fallen asleep in a chair by the bedside. He said he was awakened about 8 a.m. and sensed a powerful presence, which he described as the Presence of God. The preacher told me he sat up and looked at the foot of the bed where he saw "a mongrel-looking creature," similar to a dog, sitting at the foot of the bed. He said in an instant the "dog" was swept away and "beautiful white pillars appeared at the end of the bed. Between the pillars an angelic being stood facing the dying child." The angelic being then disappeared and a winged creature in glowing white stood and, with wings spread, fell upon the child. "Robert took one last gasp for breath as I pulled him to my arms and then he was dead." God had sent his angels to carry Robert to the Presence of God!

The angels did something else; they were visibly active to comfort and strengthen this man who loved God. A few hours later this pastor stood in the sacred pulpit and preached the Gospel!

The child was pronounced dead at 8:15 a.m. on Sunday morning. Let me just mention one other thing for you to think about. In the very next room, there was a death; same time, same hospital. Did Satan send his fallen angels to make a bid for the child of God? Was the "mongrel-looking" creature a fallen angel, was he swept away by God's Holy angels? Did he move to the next room to claim a soul for Satan? I do not know. I do know this happened just as I reported it to you.

I have, of course, been to visit many hospital patients. I have talked with doctors, nurses, chaplains, and administrators. There have been numerous reports of dying saints "seeing" their deceased mother and father, of wives "seeing" deceased husbands, of mothers "seeing" deceased children.

Knowing the angels can take on various forms, for they are spirits, what better way to escort a child of God into eternity? Some have told me of screaming, and of dying people "seeing" horrible frightful creatures just prior to death. Snakes and spiders are just a few examples. Are these fallen angels, demonic spirits? Is this a glimpse of eternal separation from God? Is this the beginning of Hell? I don't know.

Accounts of supernatural visions at death are all about us. It would seem we could draw the ultimate truth from this. At death nothing matters but knowing Jesus! Have you received the Lord Jesus into your life as your personal Savior? If God were to release angels of death to your home today, who will show up, holy angels or demon spirits? Where will they take you? Heaven or Hell?

Hell was created for the "Devil and his angels" (Matt. 25:41). The only thing separating you from that "appointment with death" is time. What is separating you from Jesus? My message is: "For God so loved the world that he gave His only begotten Son, that whosoever believeth in Him shall not perish, but have everlasting life" (John 3: 16).

Jesus did not die for the angels; He died for you and me.

My message is Jesus! But in that message, now I must include the workings of His Holy angels, for they come with redemption. Believers, be encouraged, we are a "spectacle" to the angels. They are ready to move in our lives because of Jesus. I'm glad I belong to Him.

The blood of Jesus, shed 2,000 years ago, makes me clean today. The songwriter says, "His blood will never lose its power." There are songs that we believers can sing, that the angels cannot: "Redeemed, How I Love to Proclaim It"; "Nothing but the Blood"; "Amazing Grace"; "Power in the Blood"; and a host of others!

Can you join the redeemed chorus now? Have you been redeemed'?

Chapter 9

MEANINGFUL MISSIONS

Rev. 5:2 *And I saw a strong angel proclaiming with a loud voice, who is worthy to open the book, and to loose the seals thereof?*

The angels will be active in God's judgment! We know they are active even now carrying out God's program as they are directed. Look again at the Scripture above. A strong angel is asking in a loud voice, echoing through the heavens, and I hear it on earth. Do you hear the question? Who is worthy? No man in earth or heaven was found worthy. No angel, not Gabriel, nor the cherubim or the seraphim were worthy. Perhaps Michael, the archangel, no, he is not worthy. None of God's creation was found worthy, none of it! But wait, one of the elders spoke to John and said, "Weep not There is one who is worthy." He is the Creator; He is Jesus! Rev. 5:9 says, "They sung a new song." Someday I will join in that song with believers throughout the ages and all of God's creation in heaven; thou art worthy. "Worthy is the Lamb..." (Rev. 5:12).

Angels are mentioned at least 66 times in this 66th book

of the Bible. Of this, I am sure, angels are found to be active throughout God's Word, from Genesis 3:24 to Rev.22:16. Jesus sent an angel to signify and seal the last page of His Holy Book.

More than money

A refund check for an overpayment came to my desk one morning, when I worked for the local electric company. I looked at the check and the address where it was to be delivered. The address did not fall into my "territory" or area of responsibility. Because I assumed the customer would appreciate getting her refund as soon as possible, I decided to deliver the check anyway. I made this my first stop for the day. I went to the door and knocked as usual, but did not get the usual reception. An elderly black woman came to the door and said, "You're the one." I said almost jokingly, "I suppose so. I have a refund check for you." She took the check and didn't even look at it. She put it on a table near the door and invited me in. She began to explain why she had said, "You're the one."

The woman told me she had been physically unable to attend church for a couple of years. She was old and could barely walk. She told me of how she had faithfully served the Lord for many years. Recently she said, "Two men have been coming by on Sunday afternoons. They have confused me; they call themselves Jehovah's Witnesses but they tell me I won't see Jesus when I die. They tell me I won't go to heaven." Then she said, "My eyes are bad and I can no longer read, but I can pray. I asked the Lord to send me someone to tell me the truth about Jesus and I know you're the one."

Now, I was sure, I was the one. I told of Jesus' promises to believers, of eternal life, shared scriptural promises, and had prayer with her. I read I John 5:10 and 11 to her and she was elated. Circumstances, coincidence, what would man use to rationalize this situation? Did God send His angels? Why did she overpay her bill by mistake? Why did the check come to my desk by mistake? How did she know "I was the one?" I look back on this and see God's angels at work in answer to her prayer. Yes, I believe it! I was not aware of God's angels, of prayer going up or God directing me to her home, at that time. I am now!

Similar situations

I had been invited to preach a revival meeting at the St. Paul Reformed Baptist Church where Rev. Frank Howard was pastor. I had been praying for one of my fellow office workers who by his own testimony was lost. I always invited him to wherever I might be preaching. I did not expect him to come, but asked him anyway. "Circumstances" in his life had driven him to a turning point.

Tuesday night when I arrived at this church, my friend was already there. He was searching; all he needed was Jesus. I preached about Jesus, for there is no other message. The time came for me to extend an invitation. As God's people sang and prayed I could sense the struggle in his life. I felt certain he was ready to accept Christ, but something happened. The phone rang, again and again...you could hear it from the pastor's office and it was somewhat disruptive. The pastor's wife went to the office to answer. My heart sank, it seemed the spirit was quenched. In my mind, I blamed Satan. My friend was not saved, no one was. The phone ruined everything.

Before the benediction was given, the pastor's wife announced that a lady had called and requested prayer. She said the woman's name was Jane Vines and she felt extremely depressed. She said she just looked in the phone book to call a Baptist church. The pastor's wife smiled and said the lady didn't realize she was calling a black church and was surprised when she told her they had a "white" evangelist. But she did request our prayers.

After church, I asked if she had gotten the address. "No, I just didn't think to do that," said the pastor's wife. I intended to visit the woman the next day. I felt certain I could get her address at work. The next morning, my lost friend even helped me look for the address. Our efforts failed.

We tried the city directory, a criss-cross reference telephone book; we could not find her address. My friend said, "I don't guess God intended for you to visit her." "I guess not," I said. "I sure don't know where she lives."

Angels on the job

I went to my desk where my secretary had placed the names and addresses of customers to be contacted for the day. On the top of the contact sheets was a request for a voltage check. The customer's name...Jane Vines, and of course, her address was there also. I took the order and placed it in front of my lost friend. He said, "I don't believe it!" What he meant was he couldn't help but believe it.

I went to the home of Jane Vines, now one of my dearest friends. I checked the voltage and prepared to leave. I knew I had to say something but the opportunity had not yet arisen. The elderly saint of God said, "I had the strangest thing happen last evening." She continued to tell of how she felt so low and depressed she had to have prayer by God's people. She told me she was intrigued by the name of a church as she looked through the phone book. "It seemed to stand out!" she said. "It was the Greater St. Paul Reformed Baptist Church and to top it off, it was a black church and they were in revival with a white evangelist." "Would you remember the evangelist's name if you heard it," I asked? I told her my name again. She looked at me silently as tears came streaming from her eyes. Then she burst forth with praise for God's goodness. We had prayer and I left.

That evening at church, my friend was there again when I arrived. I preached about Jesus. The invitation came and so did my lost friend! Praise God! He poured out his heart, let Jesus come into his life, and was gloriously saved. Did the angels play a part in this experience? Did they visit Jane Vines? Why did she call my office the day before? Why was my lost friend exposed to all of God's mysterious workings? Yes, I believe God set His Holy angels in action. "There is joy in the presence of the angels of God over one sinner that repenteth" (Luke 15: 10). When this man let Jesus into his life, I knew this had happened.

Angels of God are active today

I feel certain that many of God's children could relate situations where the angels were obviously at work. Why don't we talk more of the angels of God? Isaiah saw in his vision that the "Earth is full of His glory." People are skeptical and we don't want to be doubted. We don't want to be "religious nuts." We don't hear others talk about them. We know people will raise their eyebrows. My question is, "So what?" Jesus made them, they are His angels and He is my Savior. The Apostle Paul said, "I am not ashamed of the Gospel." Angels are a part of it!

Angels misrepresented

There are so many songs about angels that reveal man's ignorance about them. I hear words and lines of songs that remind me of our ridiculous ideas about angels. "She must have been a fallen angel," "Kiss an angel in the morning," and the all time favorite, "I didn't know God made honky-tonk angels."

God did make them

God made everything that is made by the Lord Jesus Christ, but He did not make fallen angels. He made angels and some fell. Thank God, He made angels with a choice; they could have been puppets. So could man, but he put within us the freedom of choice. Have you ever made a choice? You have only two, but God will honor your choice. You may choose Hell by refusing to trust Jesus, or you may choose Heaven by choosing to trust Jesus.

As you look about you, what do you see? Do you see life? God created it! Do you see the so-called "inanimate" objects about you? God created all ingredients! Do you see angels? Do you see their workings?

A few years ago my wife, Peggy, was scheduled for an operation. Plastic surgery was necessary to relieve pain when she moved her arm in various ways. I did not understand medically all that was to be done, but it was a delicate surgical procedure. Her parents had come from Atlanta to be with her for the surgery. I went with her parents early in the morning to be with her. Time passed, and she was not taken in at the scheduled hour. The surgeon was in emergency surgery. Hours passed, nurses, came to apologize and explain. It was a very unusual day some 10 hours had passed and still my wife waited. The surgeon continued to have emergencies, all day! Peggy was finally taken into surgery about 10 p.m. While she was going into surgery, after the doors were closed, another emergency. A child had somehow caught his bare foot in the wheel of his bicycle and needed immediate attention. The same doctor took the little child and tenderly, skillfully attended to him.

At 11:30 p.m., some 14 hours after being scheduled for surgery, Peggy was operated on by this same doctor; he had been in surgery continually since 9:00 a.m. I was weary from waiting. My eyes were tired from just being there. I wondered how this man could possibly do what he was doing. Surely he was tired and not as alert as he should be.

Some time after the midnight hour he came from the operating room and took me to my wife's bedside. He assured me she was just fine. Did God's angels strengthen this man? I did not see one, but in retrospect I can see they were there. They are all about us. I believe they strengthen doctors, presidents, and empower men whom in God's sovereignty, He deems in need of angelic strength. Angels are active in America.

When you want to question, believe!

I know there are multitudes of unanswered questions. Why doesn't God...? Why didn't God...? Etc.? I don't know; no one else does. Christians, my reason for writing is not to raise questions but to increase your faith in God and His plan and program. Read the Biblical accounts of angels with your spiritual eyes and see them working. Believe God's Words concerning angels.

Chapter 10

MEDITATING MINDS

I Peter I:12 *Unto whom it was revealed, that not unto themselves, but unto us they did minister the things, which are not re- ported unto you by them that have preached the gospel unto you with the Holy Ghost sent down from heaven; which things the angels desire to look into.*

By now you realize that I have talked to numerous people concerning angels. I want to share just some of what I have heard them say, and some of what I have read. I will relate some of the thoughtful answers given to me in response to questions about the angels. The meditating minds of men that I have probed lead me to arrive at two conclusions:

(1) Man's mind either magnifies his Maker or;
(2) He makes "mockery" of his Maker.

Some of these thoughts will come from news articles. I will also share the thoughts of preachers, red and yellow, black and white, educated and unlearned, liberal and conservative, with both small and large pastorates; psychiatrists, non-believers, Jewish and combination scientist-psychiatrists; law-people from all walks of life; housewives, not unlike your next door neighbor, average people.

Hopefully, we can catch a glimpse of the broad scope of opinions concerning angels from these people. I did. The more I discuss God's mighty angelic host with men, the more I am encouraged. Not many people have seen angels. Not many people even talk of the angels.

Have You ever see an angel?

Remarkably, as I have asked this question of various people, many said, "Yes." They did not always know how to talk about it and, because they felt others would not believe them, they kept it to themselves. Seldom did anyone talk with me about angels while others were present. They seemed confident that I believed in the ministry of angels. At least six people told me, without question, that what they saw was an angel from God. They were certain. They candidly described the Holy beings. Many, many people told me of "second hand" experiences. They knew someone who had told them of angelic appearances. "My grandmother" told me..., "An uncle" told me.... "A friend" told me..., etc. Statements such as this are very common. I have collected the thoughtful remarks made by a variety of people. Some are detailed; some are brief.

Preachers

Questions: "Do you believe angels are active in the lives of men today? Have you ever seen an angel?
Answers:
(1) "Yes, I believe it by faith, I believe angels are ministering spirits as the Bible declares in Hebrews

1:14. No, I have not seen with my eye any angels, but I have sensed their workings."

(2) "Yes, I believe angels are active and will be as long as God lets man remain on earth. No, I haven't seen an angel. I have talked with people who say they have."

(3) "Yes, I believe they are. I believe the Bible and I, too, have seen angels. They have appeared to me in various forms and on various occasions."

(4) "Yes, I believe they are; I don't understand their workings, but yes, I believe it. No, I have never seen one."

(5) "Oh yes, I am quite certain the angels still move at God's direction. I have never seen an angel, but somehow, by some means, God has strengthened me when I needed strength to preach. Perhaps it was the Holy Spirit, but I believe the angels' ministry includes strengthening" (see Luke 22:32).

Now these five answers are not selected answers, for not one preacher told me he did not believe in the ministry of angels today! Rather, they are represent-ative of the many with whom I spoke. Again, let me remind you the range of preachers included, from a highly educated Catholic Priest to a humble uneduc-ated pastor of a small black congregation. Perhaps you are not surprised that preachers responded with such affirmation. I am a preacher, and I was surprised.

Psychiatrists

The following article appeared in the *Dallas Morning News*. The article carried this headline, "Dead tell

113

Experiences" and was written and compiled by Helen B. Callaway.

What is it like to die? Dr. Raymond A. Moody, Jr. of Augusta, Georgia has interviewed in detail some 50 people who were clinically dead (no heartbeat, pulse or blood pressure) or at death's door. Modern science brought them back to life. Almost all of them told Moody strikingly similar stories of that "dying" experience. About 15 elements of the experience were recalled over and over by different people, Dr. Moody said. From the 50 interviews, he constructed this composite experience of dying:

"As the dying man reaches the point of greatest physical distress, he hears his doctor pronounce him dead. Then he hears a loud ringing or buzzing noise, and at the same time feels himself moving swiftly through a long dark tunnel or cylinder. Suddenly, he finds himself outside his own physical body; he sees his body from a distance, watching the resuscitation as an emotional spectator.

Presently he notices he now has a new body of a very different nature from the physical body he left behind. Then he sees the spirits of friends and relatives who have died. Next, a being of light, a warm spirit of a type he has never seen before, appears. The light spirit, without using words, asks him to evaluate his life, and shows him an instantaneous playback of his life's major events. Then he approaches some kind of boundary, apparently the line between earthly life and the beyond. He is told he must go back to earth, that his time of death has not yet come. He is told the purpose of life is to acquire knowledge and especially to learn how to love other people.

But he resists. Intense feelings of joy, love, peace, overwhelm him. He doesn't want to go back. But somehow he reunites with his physical body, and lives. Later, he tries to tell other people but can find no words to really describe the experience. He also finds that other people scoff at him, so he clams up. But the experience profoundly affects his life, and his feelings about death."

Who is this Dr. Moody, and is he kidding? He is a scientist and he is quite serious. He holds a Ph.D. in Philosophy from the University of Virginia, and in a few days will receive his M.D. degree from the Medical College of Georgia, to be followed by three years as a resident in psychiatry. His book carries a Foreword by world famous Swiss psychiatrist Dr. Elizabeth Kubler-Ross, author of *On Death and Dying* and a widely acknowledged expert in the field of death research.

Her independent studies in Illinois have established findings very similar to Moody's. Moody said one striking aspect of his research was that everyone he interviewed believed their dying experience was unique, because they had not heard of other such experiences.

All 50 original subjects were reluctant to talk even to him, but finally agreed after being assured they would remain anonymous. "I have recently lectured on this to many groups, and nearly always someone will approach me afterward to tell me of his own experience with near-death," said Moody. "I am overwhelmed with how common this experience is, and yet how little is ever heard of it."

Now, before I share a personal interview with a psychiatrist, let me comment on the preceding article. It relates to angels, because angels are directed by God to come for the dying.

I don't know the spiritual status (lost or saved), of Dr. Moody, Elizabeth Kubler-Ross, or the author of this article. This would be valuable information. However, let's assume they are completely unbiased in their reporting of such feelings.

Note the scriptural truths. The "dark tunnel or cylinder" mentioned is seen throughout the Scripture in phrases such as, "Yea, though I walk through the valley of the shadow of death..." In Luke, chapter 16, Jesus tells of the death of Lazarus and the rich man. Lazarus died and was carried by the angels into Abraham's bosom; the rich man died, and Jesus said, "In Hell, he lifted up his eyes..." Lazarus and the rich man recognized each other, but they were separated by a great gulf that could not be spanned. They were not dying; they were dead. They had passed through that "dark tunnel or cylinder!"

Jesus raised at least three people from the dead. There is no Scripture concerning their life after having known death, but Jesus did put life back into their physical bodies. He breathed the breath of life into man at his creation. It is no marvel to me that He can still speak life back into a dying body. I'm glad science is discovering this truth!

"A body of a different nature..." "Flesh and blood cannot inherit the kingdom of God." The Bible says, "This mortal must put on immortality." He sees the spirits of friends and relatives; the Scripture says, "We shall know as we are known." I'm still not surprised. "A being of light, a warm spirit," is this the angel of God? The description is scriptural. "Instantaneous playback..." All deeds are recorded whether they be good or bad and Scripture indicates both saved and lost will be rewarded or judged according to their works. Salvation is not the question here; it is the degree of reward in heaven, or degree of punishment in hell! Read II Corinthians 5:10 for the saved; then Luke 12:48 and Revelation 20: 11-15 for the lost.

"Approaches some kind of boundary." Jesus drew the line at Calvary and it extends through eternity. "Told to go back to earth..." here two scriptural possibilities exist. (1) God's grace allows the breath of life to continue so the person may come to know Jesus. (2) God allows the redeemed to see a glimpse of glory in order to tell the importance of knowing Jesus. It is by God's permission either way. These are the accounts of the dying, not the dead! "He tries to tell others...no words to describe." It is probable that the Apostle Paul, when stoned and left for dead, had a similar experience. "Intense feelings of joy, peace and love" ...already they are fruits of the Holy Spirit in the lives of believers, how much more then (Galatians 5:22). "Reluctant to talk about it." This has been my finding, too, in the discussion of angels. Those who have had supernatural experiences do not glory in them, or boast of them. God's presence in such an experience makes it so special you must keep it for yourself.

I believe the angels are very active at the time of death and this article does not lend weight to my belief in the Bible. My knowledge of God's word causes me to accept this article with a sense of "What did you expect to find?" "God's word will remain true." I regret that Jesus was left out of the findings. The most important item is missing; Jesus is the Door to Heaven! At that "boundary line" between this "life and beyond" is the blood of Jesus and you must cross that line before death!

Personal interview with a psychiatrist

I spent the afternoon in the office of a noted; well respected Doctor of Medicine and Psychiatry. He had very graciously granted me an interview to discuss angels and the "mystical phenomena." Now this man is not a Christian, he is a "Reformed Jew." He is a member of Judaism by choice; he is a Jew by birth.

He admittedly does not believe in heaven or life after death as the Bible teaches. His approach to treating the mentally ill is strictly medical. I mentioned the findings of Doctor Moody and Doctor Kubler-Ross. He was not aware of their findings and not impressed with what I reported to him. So we are now going to hear from a non-believer. I will report to you his response to my questioning on angels. I asked if he believed in the ministry of angels today? He said that he did, but did not think "revelation" had to be seen or heard. He told me of Old Testament accounts of angels, and mentioned that he understood them to be messengers. Please bear in mind that this man is speaking from a questioning, probing mind and admittedly does not believe the Bible, even the Old Testament, to be the true Word of God.

I asked if he had patients tell of seeing or hearing what they described to be angelic beings. "Yes," he said. "Hallucination is very common and these people who have told me such were always psychotic" *(a mental disorder in which the personality is very seriously disorganized-Webster's Dictionary)*. This psychiatrist said plainly, any visible or audible visions are to be understood as hallucination and psychotic. Then I asked him how he explained situations such as mentioned earlier, for example, the five-year-old girl in Oklahoma who was awakened by an angel and told that their home was on fire. Her family was saved because of this. Major news services carried the account. The event was reported by radio and newspapers; I still have the article.

He said there is a mystical force that he knows is working and would not deny the possibility of it being an angel in this case. Further, he said this type of happening is not to be confused with E.S.P. This unbelieving psychiatrist says, "Yes, I believe "some-thing," perhaps Divine, does work in the lives of men today."

It is worthy of mention that a man who deals daily with the minds of others, both lost and saved, cannot deny the work of God's Holy angels. Though he may not know how to define it, he is quite aware of a presence that "might be the hand of God." It might be angels working. Frankly, if a person does not believe God's Word there is little left for him to believe. A truth we can draw from here is, if you believe the Bible, you will believe in angels. If you don't believe the Bible, you must honestly admit that something beyond our comprehension is working in the lives of believers! Angels are alive and active in America!

"Are they not all ministering spirits sent forth to minister *for* them who shall be heirs of salvation?" Commit that verse to your scriptural memory bank and claim it often. Hebrews 1:14.

Angels, ministering to redeemed, blood-bought believers bring glory to God. Jesus is pre-imminent! God must receive the glory due Him. Hebrews 1:6 closes with the statement, "And let all the angels of God worship Him." As angels minister to me, because I belong to Jesus, they give glory to God. Angels come into our lives because of Jesus. Without Jesus, there is no promise to claim. Without Jesus the angels cannot minister. Why do I say this? All Holy angels are sent forth to minister for believers. **Sent** ...by Holy direction, **for heirs of salvation.**

Angels in outer space

Are there angels in space, or on other planets? Man has forever asked if there is intelligent life on other planets. Of course, they were speaking of life, as we know it. However, think just a moment about the few men who have been privileged to go beyond our atmosphere, even to the moon. I want to share with you some quotes from an interesting article I read recently.

A veteran of the longest manned voyage in space, Astronaut William R. Pogue, says he wanted a more challenging assignment. So he turned to Christian evangelism. He is the latest of several astronauts who have taken up work of a religious nature in the wake of their space experience.

I wonder what Astronaut Pogue saw "out there" or sensed "out there" to turn him to work for Jesus? Certainly God's

Presence is there; perhaps the angels ministered to him during this undoubtedly trying experience. At any rate, angels or not, God's presence brought this man to the most important work in earth, telling others about Jesus. Quoting from this article: "Pogue joined the staff of High Flight, an evangelistic organization founded in 1972 by another astronaut James B. Irwin. Irwin says his visit to the moon constituted a 'spiritual awakening' for him." Others told of similar reactions.

There has been a tremendous change, very quietly, in the attitudes and lives of the men who have gone to the moon, where they can see the planet the way God must (see) have seen it (the planet being earth). It is strange that only when man left his world behind could he see it for the first time. Most of the men who came back had a spiritual experience. Are angels ministering in space? If "heirs of salvation" are in space, angels are there, ready to minister. And I am convinced they travel much faster than our "rubber band" rockets. Surely our space feats are feeble in comparison to any of God's.

Werner Von Braun says the "wideness of a creator is so overwhelming. I just can't envision this whole universe corning into being without something like a divine will. I cannot envision the creation without the concept of a creator."

Astronaut Pogue said, "There's more to life than the body and intellect, it's the soul," he says. "There's that kernel that most of us miss." Now to be sure, the work of conviction is the work of the Holy Spirit, but look, if you will, with your spiritual eyes. Were the angels ministering in space? I believe so, without doubt.

The *Ft Worth Star Telegram* article quoted further, saying this about a moon trip. "The experience has to make a man truly appreciate the creation of God, the infinite precision with which God controls the universe. I could feel God's presence." Former astronaut Frank Borman has said he saw "evidence that God lives." Angels are active in assisting God in controlling the universe. They also are active in glorifying God to make man aware that "God lives." "The most beautiful and profound emotion we can experience is the sensation of the mystical. It is the source of all true science. He to whom this emotion is a stranger, who can no longer wonder and stand rapt in awe, is as good as dead."

Who said that? Read the last quote again. The late Albert Einstein said that! "Experience," "Emotion," "Mystical" ...these are his words. Angels, I believe, are ministering to man as never before. In a sense, that man is becoming increasingly more aware of God's supernatural presence and workings. Are there angels in outer space? Of course!

Angels minister for you...

...and me today because of Calvary! Angelic ministry prior to Jesus and His death, burial, and glorious resurrection was limited. From the earliest mention in the garden and throughout the Old Testament, the angels moved to accomplish a purpose for their Maker. Angels were dispatched to the Garden of Eden, but not to minister to Adam and Eve. Rather, the cherubim stood to prevent man's re-entry into the Garden. Angels moved to people on special occasions. It does not appear that the angels ministered to all Old Testament saints, at least, not in the sense that they do to believers after Calvary. There is no indication that the angels were "sent forth" prior to Calvary as they are to believers in Our Lord Jesus. "Are they not all ministering spirits sent forth to minister for them who shall be heirs of salvation." Look closely at that verse and thank God for Calvary. This is an amazing truth set forth in God's Word! It is because of Jesus, and a non-believer cannot understand this, regardless of his book knowledge.

I am writing this just to remind you

That angels are all about us and constantly working. Just a few days ago a minister's wife asked me if I thought angels might fit into an experience she wanted to relate. She told me of her sister who lived in Oklahoma. She said her sister told of how her 5-year-old daughter was so unusually happy one evening. She banged on pots and pans, sang, and seemed overjoyed for no apparent reason. Her mother inquired and was told by the little girl, "Tonight I get to go to heaven."

Of course, the mother didn't understand and did not pursue her questioning. That night there was a fire in the house. The parents were saved from the flames and the two children were not touched by the flames, but died, officially of asphyxiation. The mother told of the sweet expressions on the faces of both sleeping, now dead, children. How did the little 5-year-old girl know she was going to heaven? Did an angel reveal it to her? I don't know, but I feel quite certain that angels minister as such!

Just for the record

I recorded the account of my son's experience; I put it in an envelope, sealed and dated it. He was 7 years old; I mentioned this earlier. I wrote his age on the envelope in years, months, and days. He was 7 years, 7 months, and 7 days old. This means absolutely nothing to most people, and understandably so. Those who study Scripture closely, however, know that God's "perfect number" or God's number of completion is the number seven

.

Now as I wrote his age and the three sevens appeared, I became curious as to how many days he had lived. To my amazement the figure was 2,777 days. This is an item of interest! It could have been 6 years, 6 months, and 6 days. I am happy to have discovered that unusual combination. Some will find this scripturally valuable; some will scoff. I report it only because it's true, and as an item of interest.

Again, my purpose for writing is to magnify God and discuss His Glorious Creation, namely His Holy angels.

Another item of interest is that, according to Revelation 14:6, the time will come when "An angel flies in the midst of heaven, having the everlasting gospel to preach unto them that dwell on the earth...saying with a loud voice, Fear God, and give Glory to Him; for the hour of His judgment is come..." Angels preaching someday, angels announcing to them left behind:

"The hour of judgment is come."

Chapter 11

MENTIONING MORE

Acts 27:23 *For there stood by me this night the angel of God, whose I am, and whom I serve.*

Reports have continued to come to me about angels. Yesterday, a woman called and told me she was very sick. She had been awake all night and felt she was going to die. She had prayed to God and requested that He would not allow her to be crippled by a stroke, or left as a "vegetable." She has heart trouble and is very old. In a trembling voice, she quoted the above Scripture: "For there stood by me this night the angel of God, whose I am, and whom I serve." She then said, "I know God will provide me with dying grace when it is time for me to die." She said, "I know you are studying about angels and I suppose the Lord wanted me to share this with you."

Yes, angels still stand by the side of those who belong to Jesus. Paul said, in the verse above, referring to God, "...whose I am, and whom I serve." Whose you are, and whom you serve has a great deal to do with angelic activity about you!

Little children

"Jesus loves the little children.
All the children of the world.
Red and yellow, black and white,
They are precious in His sight,
Jesus loves the little children of the world."

In my opinion, no greater truth has ever been spoken. Jesus loves the little children! He compared the Kingdom unto little children. Lovable little children filled with faith, love, trust, and innocence. Some of the greatest joys of my ministry have been telling the little children about Jesus. They are so ready to love Him and trust Him. I see faith manifested in their little lives. I know that in heaven *their* angels do always behold the face of the Father (Matt. 18:10).

I have talked with children from all walks of life. I have seen the little black children come to know Jesus. I have seen a host of little white children come to know the Savior. I have talked with the little brown children and they too, received Jesus. The little children mirror a little bit of heaven when I see them. I have asked many of them if they would like to see an angel. All said yes, but this is what is amazing, some told me that they had already seen angels. Somehow, through God's Amazing Grace, little children are more ready to believe, more ready to see, all that God wants for them. I thank God for the little children! It is a sad transition when little children grow into the big children that we call adults. They are then not so quick to believe. As I write, study, and pray about God's message concerning angels, I become increasingly more aware of "their presence." My family has also become more aware of their presence and activities.

Our two precious sons have had their little minds at work. Numerous questions have come, many that I cannot answer, because God's Word is silent in many areas of angelic activity. My youngest son asked just a few days ago,

"Dad, do angels eat?"

I asked him to go get his Bible and read Psalm 78:25, which says, "Man did eat angels food; he sent them meat to the full." He came back to me and said it looks like they eat meat. Now I really don't know if "spirits" need to eat, but I know eating will be a part of heaven. I am satisfied that angels eat and at least in this case, mankind can eat their food. My other son said, "Dad, I don't want you to think I didn't listen to the sermon, but guess how many songs in our song book talk about angels?" We were on our way home from church. I thought back over the service and remembered a line I had sung so often, "...where bright angels feet have trod..." I knew this must have stimulated his interest. He said, "Of the first one hundred songs, seventeen of them have the word angel somewhere in the song." Stir your mind to think of God's Holy angels and their presence.

Men from all walks of life

A fellow worker told me of God's healing power in the life of his wife, Carol. She had surgery, serious surgery, and a negative outcome seemed certain. He told me he prayed and believed God, as he never had before. He said, "Now, I don't know how God did it, whether by angels assisting the surgeon or the Holy Spirit giving them wisdom or simply by God speaking, but I do know she was miraculously healed. It may have been an angel of God."

Melvin Russell was a deacon at the First Baptist Church in Burleson, Texas. I spoke recently with a prominent lawyer (who prefers to remain anonymous), from Dallas. He is a Catholic. I asked him about angels. He said, "Have I ever seen what?" I said, "Have you ever seen an angel, heard of others who have, or had an experience you would attribute to angels?" "Yes," he said, "but you really should talk with my mother, she is from the old country and she really believes in angels." He further related that she had talked of numerous times when angels of God appeared or intervened in her life. Regarding his own life, he thought for some while and then related several experiences during World War II when he should have been killed, but wasn't. He said, "In retrospect, I suppose God's angels were working in my life. I am alive and I should have been dead." He then told of plane crashes, half of his squadron being killed, but "for some reason," he wasn't. "Yes," he said, "I believe angels still work in today's world."

Floyd Jones, owner of Star Electric in the Dallas-Fort Worth area has told of angels ministering in his Christian life. He told of a preacher who refused to die when his stomach was eaten with cancer; literally eaten; to the point of the skin being laid open. He said the dying saint simply told those around him that God's angels had told him he would not die. The doctors said he had no chance. The nurses could not even go into the room because "it was so horrible looking." The stomach wound was healed. The cancer disappeared. The man lived and walked away from that hospital. God's angels cannot fail, because God cannot fail. With tear-filled eyes, he shared this experience and said, "I wish more people would tell of God working in their lives." I do too! His Holy angels are busy today!

Reports continue to come to me

I suppose I have "ended" this book at least four or five, times, only to find more must be written. Someone hears of my interest in angels and testimonies begin to come my way. I am grateful. I mentioned the newspaper account of the little 5-year old girl in Foyil, Oklahoma to a group of deacons at our church. One of the men told me he knew the family personally. He told in detail of what really happened. The little girl was asleep in one end of their mobile home; her parents were asleep in the opposite end. A fire broke out in the center of the mobile home and the flames separated her from her sleeping parents. She said her angel awakened her and told her to go and tell her parents that their home was on fire. The child told of how the beautiful white angel held back the flames so she could get through the small passageway.

Further, the deacon said, "Reporters tried to confuse her by crisscrossing her with questions for hours, but her story did not change." She knew what had happened. He also mentioned that this has had a tremendous impact upon the spiritual lives of that family, their loved ones, and friends. The reporters were convinced "enough" for the story to make the major wire services. God's supernatural work is worthy of reporting! However, His Holy angels do not have to make the headlines to cause me to see them at work!

During this same discussion, another of the men, Virgil Armstrong, asked if I had heard Ken Copeland's testimony regarding angels. I do not know Ken Copeland, but I did recognize his name when I was told that he was an evangelist. The man told me that Brother Copeland had testified to seeing his "personal" angel on numerous occasions, and he described him as being over 10 feet tall. I believe that. In this same discussion, I was told of a testimony given the night before at a Christian fellowship meeting. The story concerned six Russian believers who were being persecuted by the Communists in Russia. The men were given a choice, to recant and denounce Jesus, or to meet a slow cruel death. The six believers chose to stay with Jesus. They would not denounce Him! Consequently, they were taken to a frozen lake, or pond, told to undress and walk around the pond until they froze to death. Still the bold believers would not recant. Five of the men had died and the sixth was near death when a Russian soldier beckoned him to the fire where they stood warming themselves. According to the testimony, the soldier said, "Let me die for you." The believer said, "I don't understand, aren't you a Communist? A Russian Communist soldier?" "Yes," he said, "but I have seen the other five die. I saw a beautiful white glowing being come for each of the other five: He placed a crown upon each of their heads and carried them away. I want to die in your place."

I report this to you, just as it was reported to me. Yes, I believe it, because I believe God's Word.

Another church member told me of two girls walking home after dark. Several teenage boys began following them. As the boys got closer, they made obscene remarks and threatened to seize the girls by force if they would not go with them voluntarily. The frightened girls walked faster and were about to scream, when suddenly the boys stopped following; they retreated and left in the opposite direction.

Later, one of the boys told the girls at school that he was one of those involved. He apologized. One of the girls asked why they stopped so suddenly, and what caused them to run away? "We were so frightened," he said. "It was those two big guys walking beside you. Where did they come from?" The girl replied, "There was no one with us, no one at all." "Oh yes," he said. "We all saw them and they were big guys!" Were they God's angels? I have no problem believing the accounts of angelic ministries. The more I study and listen to testimonies of God's children, the more encouraged I am.

Think about it

In the same discussion with these men I mentioned that I still had never seen an angel. "How do you know you haven't?" said one of the men. "How can you be sure, in light of Hebrews 13:2?" I smiled as I thought of the Scripture, that says we may "...entertain angels unawares..." Interesting thought.

A few days later I sat in the study of one of the most respected preachers in the state of Texas, a man who pastors one of the landmark churches in the city of Fort Worth. He has entertained foreign diplomats at the request of our Presidents; he has preached at the nation's largest conventions; I talked with him about angels. I didn't have too much to say. He said, "Not everyone believes that angels still minister today, but I certainly do." He then told of an experience he had while in high school. His father was pastor of a church and he had four brothers who also were preachers. He said, "In my mind, I was determined just to be a regular fellow, get a job and a family." He described the parsonage where he lived in Austin, Texas. He mentioned outside stairs that led to his room upstairs. He told me that when his high school girl friend would come to see him, she would always jump onto the steps and he could hear her coming. He also mentioned that she died just prior to the event he was about to relate.

He told me he had arrived home from a very tiring football practice. "I took a hot shower and was relaxing on my bed when I heard that same 'jump' on the staircase that I had heard so many times before. I got up and looked, but, of course, I knew it could not be her." He said he went back to the bed and in an instant she appeared in the form of an angel. "She was there just for a fleeting moment, then she was gone." He told me he did not understand it all, but something from that "angelic appearance" tugged at him until he gave his life to the ministry of the Gospel. Rev. L. B. George, Pastor of the historic Mt. Zion Baptist Church said, "Some folks don't believe that God still speaks and ministers to man through His mighty angels, but Brother Don, I sure do. I sure do!"

Rev. Nehemiah Davis of the Mount Pisgah Baptist Church made some interesting comments relative to our study. He was preaching to a group of preachers at a minister's alliance meeting. His message dealt with the Doctrine of the Trinity. In his preaching, he spoke of not understanding the Trinity. He said, "I have never seen God the Father, God the Son, nor God the Holy Spirit. But," he said, "Though I have never seen them, nor understood them, I still believe by faith that *They Are!*" He told of his salvation experience. He told that when he was young it was necessary to have "seen something in the cornfield" before you could be saved. He said, "I knew something was dealing with my heart, I knew I wanted to go to heaven, but I had never seen anything in the cornfield. I couldn't sleep one night, so I got up and went out to the cornfield," he said. "I begged God to let me see something, but I never did." He said he knew what he needed to do; he just hadn't seen anything yet. The next Sunday morning in church, he said, "I looked up at mama," ("Now you didn't tell your mama in those days, you asked," he smiled). "Mama, I've got to go today!" He smiled even bigger, as this highly educated black minister recalled the simple joy of that moment. He said, "My mama looked down at me with tears and said, "Watcha waitin' on boy, go ahead on.' I did and Jesus saved me, but I still haven't seen anything in the cornfield!" Amen. Physical sight is not necessary to believing. Faith in God's Word is sufficient.

I spoke with Rev. D. Evans of the Fellowship Baptist Church recently. We spoke of church matters, as you would expect. Have you ever wondered what preachers discuss when they get together? This came to my mind as I talked with this pastor. We talked about angels! I will share some of Rev. Evans's comments, but first let's back up to the question of "What do preachers talk about?"

For some reason man has placed preachers in a position that is not characteristic and not scriptural. Preachers are people, just people. They are not without fault; they are not even special people. God has placed His Hand on your life, too, if you are His Child. The roles of service are different, but preachers are just people.

Now some preachers may resent this. They will call my attention to Scripture, stating how God is pleased with preachers, etc., but I am one, I know hundreds, and we are just people, called of God to preach.

Preachers are messengers, but are not angels

Never place your faith in a preacher! You will be disappointed, for he is human just as you are. Place your faith in Jesus. He cannot disappoint you! I fear when man "lifts me up," for I know my responsibility is to "lift up Jesus." It is to point men to Him, never to me. God help the preacher, who seeks glory that belongs to God.

Rev. Evans and I discussed some of what I just shared with you. We, as every preacher, should have discovered the joy of the ministry is praising God. He can make the joy bells ring in His preacher's heart. I asked Rev. Evans if he had ever seen angels. He smiled and said, "Yes, sir, I have. Many times." I asked him to tell me of some of his experiences. "Sometimes," he said, "I get so caught up in the spirit of preaching about sweet Jesus, that while I am preaching it seems like the air is full of angels, beautiful beings. Sometimes it looks like they are inviting me to come on into the kingdom. When that happens, I just can't hold back the tears of joy; my entire soul is flooded with joy. Tears of joy have to come."

With controlled excitement he told me what I already knew. "When God chooses to let you real close to Him, when He gives you a precious glimpse of Glory, you can't tell all about it, it just makes you want to weep at His Goodness. Yes, He's Mighty Good, Mighty Good." I could only say, "Amen! He is Mighty Good!"

I honestly feel I could write forever about the angels of God, just because they are the angels of God. I have talked, I suppose, to at least one hundred different people about this subject. I could share one hundred testimonies of angelic activity. I will talk to someone tomorrow and the next day, but already by faith in God's Word, by experience, and by the testimony of others, I am convinced. I am overwhelmed at the working of angels and man's reluctance to talk about it.

Testimonies are consistent. No new revelations; God's Word is complete! Appearances follow the Biblical pattern. They appear. They speak. They disappear. They reappear. There is a heavenly touch in each experience that you cannot share with others; some of the experiences are for the individual only. Some come as an assurance. Some come as a warning. Some come to bring your attention to a segment of God's Word. Some come and minister without our knowledge, unaware. Angels bring you closer to Jesus. They seek to magnify Him. They protect, when Satan would try to destroy. They come as directed by God, in answer to prayer. They appear in a form *always* recognized as being from God. They never leave the believer confused. They are all about us.

My study and reporting to you has drawn me closer to Jesus than I thought possible in this life. With my physical eye I have still never seen an angel; perhaps someday God will give me a glimpse. It is not necessary to my faith in Him or His Word because, with my spiritual eyes, I see more of God's glory than ever before. Angels, I believe, read as I am writing. I am confident if they brought me a message from God's throne to close this book it would be similar to that of Rev. Evans, "He's Mighty Good...Mighty Good!"

Chapter 12

MESSENGERS OF MERCY

The time had come for the greatest announcement of man's history. The long awaited Messiah was to be born of a woman. God's Son was about to lay aside His Heavenly garments, to take upon Himself the form of a man and to be born of a woman.

Someone had to announce to the people that Jesus was coming; a "forerunner" had to tell the people that the King was on His way. God sent an angel to tell man what message was to be delivered.

Luke's account tells us that the priest, Zacharias, was in the Temple, performing his priestly duties when, without warning, "there appeared unto him an angel of the Lord..." (Luke 1:11). Zacharias was frightened, for, without any prior knowledge or expectation, God's angel appeared unto him. Zacharias saw him! The angel calmed him, saying, "Fear not." As you read this account in Luke, note these things that happened.

1. Zacharias was in the temple serving God (v. 8).

2. He had prayed. God sent an angel to answer his prayer (v. 13).

3. The angel told of future events (v. 13).

4. The angel brought the name for the child (v. 13).

5. Zacharias saw the angel (v. 12).

6. He conversed with him (v. 18). He questioned him.

7. The angel introduced himself (v. 19).

8. He pronounced judgment because of Zacharias' doubt (v. 20).

What can be concluded? The angel moved as God commanded; and it was in response to Zacharias' prayer to be used of God. He had an experience that skeptics could doubt; but he would never be the same again. For at least nine months Zacharias could not speak, just as the angel had pronounced. In verse 63, when the child was born, Zacharias was able to speak; and he named the child as directed by God's *marvelous messenger,* "...His name is John."

Messiah in the manger

God's *marvelous messengers* were busy as the time drew near. Six months after Gabriel was sent to Zacharias, he was dispatched from the presence of God to a woman named Mary to announce the miraculous birth of God's Son (Luke 1:26).

Again we see a hint of the angels' workings. Gabriel goes unannounced to Nazareth, to the home of Mary. He appears and greets her with a message from God's throne. Mary, too, was afraid (v. 29) but, as Zacharias, Mary was told to, "Fear not." As God sent the name for John, he did for Jesus (Luke 1:31). Once more let us learn something from this angelic experience in Luke's first chapter.

1. Gabriel was sent (v. 26).
2. He appeared suddenly (v. 28).
3. He spoke (v. 28).
4. She saw him (v. 29).
5. Her fear was turned to comfort (v. 30).
6. Future events were revealed unto her (v. 30-33).
7. She questioned him (v. 34).
8. She received an assuring answer (v. 35).
9. She was given news of Zacharias and Elizabeth (v. 36).
10. The Angel proclaimed, "For with God nothing shall be impossible" (v. 37).

And as is the case throughout scriptures, the angel departed from her (v. 38). It seems that in a fleeting moment the angels can descend from God's presence, deliver His message, and return. Billy Graham said, "They appear. They speak. They reappear."

Additionally, God had not forgotten about Joseph. Would he have believed Mary had she told him of the message sent by an angel; that the Holy Spirit would conceive in her; and she would be the mother of God's Son? Would you? He was a just man (Matt. 1:19), and knowing she was pregnant was still prepared to take her as his wife; surely his mind and heart were troubled. While he thought on these things (v. 20) "the angel of the Lord appeared unto him in a dream..." Was he awake? Was this a vision or a visitation as Mary and Zacharias had? Notice that verse 24 indicates Joseph was asleep. The angel of the Lord appeared in a dream. Let's look closer:

1. Joseph was troubled before the angel came (Matt. 1:19-20).
2. God knew this and dispatched "the angel of the Lord," who here is nameless (v. 20).
3. He was given a heavenly message (v. 20).
4. Was told what to name the child (v. 21).
5. Was assured this was in keeping with the Scripture (v. 23) (the angels never speak contradictory, nor contrary to God's written word).
6. Joseph, too, had assurance from heaven (v. 24).

There is more that we can learn from the angel's activity when the Savior of man was born. (Remember, Jesus did not die for fallen angels but for fallen man.) See our books on demons and deliverance to learn more about fallen angels, but let's take a glimpse at their activity here by way of speculation.

There are two classes of angels: God's holy angels who cannot fall or fail; and those angels who, by their choice, fell in Lucifer's rebellion against the Almighty (see Isa. 14:12). They, too, were busy as the baby Jesus was born, working in the hearts of sinful man. What caused Herod to be troubled when he received news of Jesus' birth? What caused him to want to destroy God's son? (Matt. 2:3,13).

The same fear that came upon Pharaoh when Moses was born (Israel's Deliverer) now came upon King Herod. The fallen angels, Satan's host of evil spirits, were seeking to destroy Jesus. However, God intervened and dispatched a messenger to warn Joseph and Mary of impending danger, "...they departed into their own country another way" (Matt. 2:12). While departing, "the angel of the Lord appeared to Joseph in a dream, saying, 'Arise, and take the young child and his mother, and flee into Egypt...until I bring thee Word...'"(v.1, 13).

God's Son was safe. He was not waiting for heaven to send instructions (Matt. 2:19). As promised, an angel of the Lord appeared in a dream and gave explicit instructions that led Jesus, Joseph, and Mary to Nazareth in Galilee to fulfill the Scripture (Matt. 2: 19-23). Much can be learned from this account. What has happened? An apparent spiritual confrontation of God's Holy angels and Satan's fallen angels. God's angels cannot fail because they are God's angels. They are superior because He is! Look at their activities in Matthew, chapter 2.

1. The angels warned of danger (v. 12).
2. The angels directed them from danger (v. 13).
3. The angels left a promise. "...I will bring thee word" (v. 13).
4. The angels kept their promise (v. 19).
5. The angels could not act contrary to Scripture (v. 22,23).
6. The angels in Joseph's life always appeared "in a dream."
7. There is no indication that Joseph spoke to the

angels, nor questioned the angels; he only obeyed these heavenly "messengers."

8. Angels are mentioned five times in Matthew's account of Joseph (chapter 1:20,24; 2:13,19, 22). Each came with a message from God.

Matthew and Luke record the birth and childhood of Jesus. Possibly the most complete account is found in Luke, chapter 2. Luke reminds us that angels did not only deal with priests in the temple, the chosen Mother of Jesus, and Joseph, her espoused, but they went to the shepherds (v. 8,15) watching over their flocks by night. The glory of the angels was so bright, so magnificent, the shepherds were afraid. The angel, as directed by God, spoke that great verse of Scripture so often quoted at Christmas time. "For unto you is born this day in the City of David a Saviour, which is Christ the Lord" (Luke 2:11).

Something can be learned from this angelic visitation (Luke 2:1-15).

1. The angel appeared to more than one individual (v.8).
2. The angel brought with him some of God's presence (v. 9).
3. The angel appeared unexpectedly, but character- istically calmed those to whom he appeared. "Fear not" (v. 10).
4. The angel brought only a heavenly message (v. 11- 12).
5. "Suddenly" there appeared with the angel a multitude of angels (v. 13).
6. The host of angels came unannounced, performing their heavenly duties, "praising God" (v. 13).

7. They were gone; mission accomplished (v. 5). They appeared. They spoke. They were gone.

Very little is known about the wise men from the East. I can be certain there were at least two, for reference is made in Matthew 2:1-11 with terms as "we" and "they." However, I would be more inclined to believe there were thirty wise men rather than just three. The Bible simply does not say; because there were three gifts brought to the manger, Bible students have assumed there were three wise men. That, I believe, is of little importance; what is important in our study is how did they find the Savior?

Herod demanded to know how they knew the child was born (v. 7). The "star," which they saw in the East, went before them and stood over where the young child was (v. 9). "When they saw the star, they rejoiced with exceeding great joy" (v. 10). Was an angel directing them in the form of a star? Were these men special people? If so, their names are not mentioned, not even their country. What can we learn here? (Matt.2:1-11).

1. The word angel is not mentioned.
2. No message was given to the wise men.
3. They saw and followed "something" that caused them to believe they would find Jesus.
4. Why do men think they were astrologers; they were looking for Jesus. They saw "His star" and came to "worship Him" (v. 2). Why didn't Herod's people?
5. I believe the angels were active here. The shepherds saw an angel whose glory shone in brilliance. The wise men came, apparently, months later.

I believe the "star" they followed obviously was of God and fits in with the scheme of angelic ministry. From this scriptural account we can only suppose the angels of God were active; but I believe it is a safe assumption. The greatest truth I can draw from this passage is that WISE MEN STILL SEEK HIM. And if an angel from heaven had only one message for man, I am convinced it would be "Seek him that is born king of the Jews."

I have read much, and talked with many, concerning angels as I prepared this material. The great joy is digging into the meat of God's Word and allowing Him to speak personally. I have given you milk, gleaned from many sources. I trust you will study the Scripture for yourself. For this reason I am including some thoughts and more Scripture.

In Summary:

Angel, "messenger" is used of God, of men, and of an order of created spiritual beings whose chief attributes are strength and wisdom (II Sam. 14:20; Ps. 103:20, 104:4). In the O.T. the expression "the angel of the Lord" (sometimes of God) usually implies the presence of Deity in angelic form (Gen. 16:1-23, 21:17-19, 22:11-16, 31:11-13; Ex. 3:24; Judges 2:1-6, 13:3-22). See Mal. 3:1, note. The word angel is used of men in Luke 7:24; James 2:25; Rev. 1:20; 2:1,8,12,18; 3:1,7, 14. In Rev. 8:3-5 Christ is evidently meant.

Sometimes angel is used of the spirit of man (Matt. 18:10, Acts 12:15). Though angels are spirits (Ps. 104:4; Heb. 1:14) power is given them to become visible in the semblance of human form (Gen. 19:1 of v. 5; Ex. 3:2; Num.

144

22:22-32; Judges 2:1, 6:11,22, 13:3,6; I Chron. 21:16, 20; Matt. 1:20; Luke 1:26; John 20:12; Acts 7:30, 12:7,8, etc.). The word is always used in the masculine gender though sex in the human sense is never ascribed to angels (Matt. 22:30; Mark 12:25). They are exceed-ingly numerous (Matt. 26:53; Heb. 12:22; Rev. 5:11; Ps. 68:17). Their power is inconceivable (2 Kings 19:35). Their place is about the throne of God (Rev. 5:11,7:11). Their relation to the believer is that of "ministering spirits, sent forth to minister for them who shall be heirs of salvation," and this ministry has reference largely to the physical safety and well-being of believers (1 Kings 10:5; Ps. 34:7,91:11; Dan. 6:22; Matt. 2:13, 19, 4:11; Luke 22:43; Acts 5:19, 12:7-10).

From Heb. 1:14 with Matt. 18:10, and Ps. 91:11, it would seem that this care for the heirs of salvation in infancy, continues through life. The angels observe us (1 Cor. 4:9; Eph. 3:10; Eccles. 5:6), a fact which should influence conduct. They receive departing saints (Luke 16:22). Man is made "a little lower than the angels," and in incarnation Christ took "for a little" (time) this lower place (Ps. 8:4,5; Heb. 2:6,9) that He might lift the believer into His own sphere above angels (Heb. 2:9,10). An archangel, Michael, is mentioned as having a particular relation to Israel and to the resurrections (Dan. 10:13,21; 12:2; Jude 9:1; I Thess. 4:16). The only other angel whose name is revealed, Gabriel, was employed in the most distinguished services (Dan. 8:16,9,21; Luke 1:19,26).

Fallen Angels Two classes of these are mentioned:

(1) "The angels which kept not their first estate (place)

but left their own habitation, "are chained under darkness," awaiting judgment (2 Pet. 2:4; Jude 6:1; I Cor. 6:3; John 5:22). The origin of these is nowhere explicitly revealed. They may be identical with the demons (Matt. 7:22, note).

(2) For Satan and his angels, everlasting fire is prepared (Matt. 25:41; Rev. 20:10). The Scriptures are clear about angels that rebelled against God. Judgment awaits them, but in the meantime, we, as believers fight against them as described in Ephesians 6. Please read our books about demons, *SERPENTS IN THE SANCTUARY* and *TURMOIL IN THE TEMPLE.*

We live in human bodies; our world is tangible. It enriches us when we are able to see into, or get insight into, what the Scriptures reveal as the "spirit world." There is but a step from the "natural" world to the "spirit world." The dividing veil is our "fleshly" body. They are two classes, good and evil. They are classified as "seraphim," "cherubim," "angels" (good and bad), "principalities," "powers," "rulers of darkness," "wicked spirits" (Eph. 6:12), "thrones," "dominions" (Col. 1:16), "fallen angels" (2 Pet. 2:4), "spirits in prison" (1 Pet. 3:18-20), "demons," "seducing spirits," (I Tim. 4:1).

The "seraphim" have three pair of wings. They are the attendants of the "Lord of Hosts" and call attention to His holiness (Isa. 6:1-8). The "cherubim," or "living creatures," as described in Ezekiel 1:4-25; 10:1-22, have only two pair of wings, but they have "four faces" on their head, the front face, that of a "man"; the left of a "lion"; the right of an "ox" (calf); and the back of an "eagle." They also have the "hand of a man" under their wings on each of their four sides. They are the guardians of the throne of God. The "seraphim," "cherubim," "angels," and all other heavenly beings, are created beings. They did not exist from all eternity (Col. 1: 16).

How many angels are there? The angels are "innumerable" (Heb. 12:22). They are "mighty in power," but not almighty (2 Thess. 1:7); they excel in strength. One angel destroyed 185,000 of the Assyrian army in a night. An angel rolled away the stone from the Tomb of Christ, and one angel shall bind Satan and cast him into the "bottomless pit." They are "Glorious beings" (Luke 9:26), and have great knowledge, but are not omniscient. They neither marry nor are given in marriage (Matt. 22:30). That does not mean that they are "sexless" and have not the power of procreation. All the angels in the Scriptures are spoken of as men, and were so created in great numbers, and as they do not die (Luke 20:36) there is no need for "procreation," but that they have such power seems indisputable from Gen. 6:14, where we are told that the "Sons of God" (angels, probably fallen angels) had intercourse with the "daughters of men," and the result was a race of "Mighty Men" (see chapter two on the cause of the flood). From this we see that the angels can sin. The angels are "ministering spirits" to them who are 'heirs of salvation' " (Heb. 1: 13,14), and "executioners of God's Wrath" on the "wicked" (2 Thess. 1:7-8). They will gather the "elect of Israel" from the four corners of the earth (Matt. 24:31) and are commissioned to supply the physical needs of God's people (Matt. 4:11; I Kings 19:4-8). I include these thoughts and Scripture references for those who want to study God's Word more thoroughly. These thoughts are not mine.

I think from my study of angels I can confidently say that angels have personality and emotion. I understand they may eat, they speak a heavenly language according to Paul, "Though I speak with the tongues of men and angels..." (1 Cor. 13:1). The angels are spirits, but are not limited to spirit form. They are masculine; they have no need to reproduce, for they do not age nor die. They worship God and minister to man. They can "appear" to man as God directs. They do not desire worship. They are in various degrees of rank and strength. They are mighty in power. They seem to be unlimited by time, distance, and speed, in the sense of moving from God's presence to ours in a "flash" (Isa. 6).

Gabriel pronounced judgment upon Zacharias for doubting God. They come in answer to prayer according to Daniel. Ezekiel saw some he could describe. They are "innumerable." They announce, reveal, and strengthen. They appear. They speak. They disappear. They come at death. To this point, I have said nothing I have not said earlier. There is Scripture that indicates they may possess another quality not yet mentioned. Healing power? I believe they guide surgeons' hands and move in protecting roles for our physical well-being. What about this in Scripture? "For an angel went down at a certain season into the pool, and troubled the water; whosoever then first after the troubling of the water stepped in was made whole of whatsoever disease he had" (John 5:4).

This is a mysterious verse of Scripture. "An angel" came and "troubled the waters." Whatever the angel did to the water brought healing to the first to step into the pool. It did not matter what the disease was, cold or cancer, there was healing.

From this I want to conclude that whatever an angel brings from heaven is from God: it may be a message, but it is God sent. It may be a judgment, but it is God sent. It may be revelation, but it is God sent. If the angels possess "healing powers," it is because of God. How did the people know it was an angel that "troubled the water?" I don't know, but there was no question about the healing as they stepped from the waters. Healing powers? Yes, because they are God's Holy angels and He is able to heal! Remember the Holy angels are never to be confused with the Holy Spirit. They work for Him and with Him. He is the Holy Spirit; they are spirits that are Holy because of their Holy God.

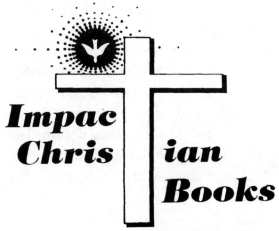

Impac Chris ian Books

332 Leffingwell Ave., Suite 101
Kirkwood, MO 63122

AVAILABLE AT YOUR LOCAL BOOKSTORE, OR YOU MAY ORDER DIRECTLY. Toll-Free, order-line only M/C, DISC, or VISA 1-800-451-2708.

Visit our Website at *www. impactchristianbooks.com*

Write for *FREE* Catalog.